Flags in Berlin

Portrait of Biddy Youngday, née Brigid Macnaghten, taken in Berlin 1930s

Flags in Berlin

An account of life in Berlin 1928–1945

Biddy Youngday

Published by Mary Brimacombe and Clara Lowy

First published 2012 by Mary Brimacombe and Clara Lowy

44A Rosemont Road, London W3 9LY

ISBN: 978–0–9571601–0–1

Printed and bound by Henry Ling Ltd, The Dorset Press, Dorchester

Contents

Preface

This book was written by Biddy Youngday, née Brigid Macnaghten. It is an account of her life in Germany 1928-1945 and in England for a year after the war.

Biddy came from a privileged background. Her father was a judge, a Unionist M.P. for Londonderry, N. Ireland and later a Privy Councillor. Her mother was the daughter of the social reformer Charles Booth. There were four children: a boy, Anthony, and three girls, Mary, Biddy and Anne.

Biddy went to the Slade School of Art and then continued her studies in Paris for three years. She decided to go to Berlin because it seemed to be the centre for new and exciting art movements.

The first part of the book describes her bohemian way of life, mixing with sculptors and artists. She became interested in politics, partly due to the growth of fascism around her and, partly due to the influence of her Bauhaus friends.

She married Willi Jungmittag, a photography student from the Bauhaus. His background was quite different. He came from a family of artisans. His father was a metal worker and his mother active in the socialist party in Bremen.

Biddy records the life of the Germans around her before and during the war. She writes about the plight of her communist and Jewish friends and acquaintances. Willi, her husband, became involved in a resistance group against the Nazis. Recent research has shown that this group, the Saefkow-Jacob-Bästlein Organisation had over 500 members from all walks of life. Sadly in the summer of 1944 almost 300 were arrested and 100 men and women were executed or died in concentration camps.

The entry of the Red Army into Berlin is described in Chapter 5 and Chapter 6 is about Biddy's journey from D.P.[1] camp to D.P. camp until she finally reaches England.

The final chapter should be compulsory reading for doctors and nurses working with mental patients. She writes about life in two mental hospitals and how she recovered from her nervous breakdown.

1 displaced person

Biddy wrote her story in the 1950's and 1960's. Copies of the manuscript have been floating around family and friends for many years, all of them saying how interesting it was.

The real stimulus to do something came in the summer of 2009. My family was invited to an exhibition, held in Berlin's Humboldt University, about the Saefkow-Jacob-Bâstlein resistance network. We met some of their families and they all had moving stories to tell. I thought it was time to do something about my mother's story.

As far as possible I have tried to keep Biddy's voice, only editing the text when the meaning was unclear and adding footnotes to provide information about the people mentioned.

My thanks to Ken Brooks for preparing the text for print, organising the photos and the final design of the cover.

Mary (Gerda) Brimacombe
2012 Quemper-Guezennec, France

Introduction

It was a long time ago, on a bright cold 30th January 1933 in Berlin.

Over the wireless came the news that Hitler was Chancellor and one after another, like magic, the swastika flags appeared from the windows, bright scarlet with a black centre. They looked rather pretty, like berries on a winter tree.

I had been living in Berlin for five years and as a result had joined the Communist Party. I came from a middle-class conservative family and had, till I came to Berlin, not been interested in politics. I was thirteen when the First World War ended. I studied Art at the Slade School in London and then spent three months in Florence. I thought fascism and Italian fascists depressing, to say the least of it. Then I went to Paris where I lived for three years. My sister Mary, who had been in New York for a year, joined me in Paris and we made up our minds to go to Germany. We had each of us an allowance from my father of £160 a year.

Biddy, art student. This photo was probably taken in Paris in the 1920's.

Chapter I Berlin 1928–1933

We arrived at the Friedrichstrasse station at night and found a room at the Hotel Atlas. It was on the top floor with a window overlooking the canal and the railway lines. I painted a picture of Berlin from it. We looked for somewhere to live, not easy when you can't speak any German. We hunted for five days, walking along the Berlin streets; the distance can sometimes be a mile between the numbers one and a hundred. In the end we found a Büro Zimmer[1] in the Potsdammerstrasse. It was rather nice with a garden and trees to look at, just by the Potsdammerbrücke. There was one room and we shared the lavatory with a firm of wool merchants. We cooked with an electric cooking pot. Mary slept on the sofa and I slept on a folding bed which we bought at Wertheims in the Potsdammerplatz. She hired a piano and practised Brahm's 'Variations on a theme by Handel' while I painted still life's of pears and chrysanthemums. For baths, we went to the public baths in the Lutzowstrasse: a depressing workhouse type of building. For friends, we went to the Romanisches café which we heard was the 'Dome' of Berlin.[2] We soon made friends. I picked up Axel who was Russian and Mary picked up Yussef who came from Palestine; he was half-Arab half-Jewish. Axel was a musician and Yussef was a sculptor.

The early autumn in Berlin is rather lovely; we went to Potsdam. The snag about the Büro Zimmer was that the central heating went off mid-day Saturday. It didn't come on again till Sunday evening. We used to sit there clutching the pipes waiting for the first feel of warmth. So when Axel asked us to tea one Sunday we were very glad. He had a room near the Kantstrasse where the window looked over a timber yard onto the railway; he was a Russian émigré. Before the revolution he lived in St. Petersburg and was a botanist, but his passion was the theatre and music. In the civil war he fought on the side of the White Russians; he fought mostly in trains. He landed up with Kolchak's army in the Crimea and when the Bolsheviks came over the ice and defeated Kolchak[3]

1 a room above an office

2 Le Dôme Café in Montparnasse, Paris, known as the Anglo-American café, meeting place for artists and intellectuals on the left bank.

3 Aleksandr Kolchak 1874-1920, leader of anti-bolshevik forces.

he was taken prisoner. By birth he was Latvian and since Latvia had become independent, he escaped there. In Russia he had a wife and a little girl. He had obtained a divorce and remarried in Riga to the niece of a wealthy business man Herr Stamm, who gave him money to go to Karlsruhe and study composition under Hindemith.[1] He was very happy there but unfortunately his wife died of tuberculosis so he came to Berlin. He still had a monthly allowance of 150 marks from Herr Stamm.

Yussef came to Berlin because he had been presented to the Kaiser who had visited Palestine before the 1914 war. Yussef was working as a young sculptor on a stone monument. He had packed all his belongings into a vast iron chest in case the ship which carried him over the Mediterranean was wrecked. It needed four strong men to carry it. I don't think the iron chest ever got to Berlin but Yussef did. He had an exhibition and did fairly well. He had a beautiful studio on the Tiergartenstrasse which he kept spotlessly clean. He was only about five foot two. He had tremendous vitality but he was also excessively vain.

Axel had tuberculosis. He was in a bad state of health and he chain smoked. One evening I went down to the Romanisches café alone because Mary had a cold. Axel was there. We sat, and sat, and sat, and in the end I went home with him. It was a very unsatisfactory love affair. He was much too ill and I was frigid. We lay together all night and watched the morning come over the snow-covered timber yard, a frosty morning with blue shadows.

Mary was living with Yussef. Both the men wanted to marry us. I didn't because I was put off of being somebody's third wife. Also Axel gave me the clap which frightened me and was very unpleasant. Mary didn't marry Yussef because she couldn't face up to the family reaction to Yussef's appearance and explosive Arabian ways. After I broke with Axel his health became much worse. He sat smoking in beer stuben all night in the Tauentzien strasse. In the end all his friends clubbed together and sent him to a sanatorium. He came out better but only for a time and he died a year later. I went and visited him in hospital where he lay in a ward for old men who were dying. He didn't seem to care much. His life had been disrupted too much and he had lost the will to live. Perhaps, if I had married him and we had gone to live in the south of France, he

1 Hindemith 1895-1963 German composer

would have been alright. Perhaps he really had lung cancer which wasn't known about in those days. Yussef came to England when Hitler came to power. He was half-Jewish. He married and had lots of lovely Arabian children but never made his name as sculptor.

I began to be interested in politics. Wall Street had crashed and unemployment had come. Some of the banks had to close their doors and there were frightened queues of people trying to get their money. On May 1st 1929 the Social Democratic chief of police banned the May Day demonstration. The German Communist Party called on the workers to demonstrate in spite of the ban so I went to the Potsdammerplatz to see what would happen. It was a nasty cold day and it was raining. There were a lot of police and demonstrators running across the road. The police were hitting them with their rubber truncheons. I saw one boy fall as he was beaten.

We made friends with a communist who was a sculptor and came from Budapest. He had taken part in the Bela Kun revolution there and when Horthy came to power he escaped, like many other Hungarians, to Berlin.[1] He had no work and was living on the dole. He had a studio very near to ours in the Potsdammerstrasse. We had moved from the Büro Zimmer. By joining the Artists trade union I was entitled to a studio.

We moved into the studio at Christmas time. It was up six unlit flights of back stairs above the offices of the Bund Deutscher Kriegs Beschädigte.[2] The studio was very small. We had a passage where we had a gas ring and did our cooking and washing. There was another tiny room with a skylight heated by a thing called a grude,[3] a horrible and primitive forerunner of an Aga stove, which smelled foul and nearly asphyxiated one. Mary had her piano in it. The Berlin piano movers, a splendid race full of deep earthy humour, had to haul it up the front stairs, through the war veteran's office, and then up the six flights of back stairs. Yussef found us a putzfrau.[4] Fraulein Zylinski was Polish, blonde and very nice. She did all our washing, including sheets, on the gas ring in the passage and hung it out to dry in the boden,[5] where we also kept

1 Bela Kun,1886-1938, leader of short lived Hungarian revolution, 1919, overthrown by right wing counter revolutionaries led by Horthy,1868-1957

2 War veteran's organisation

3 stove 4 charlady 5 attic

our coal. This was manhandled up the six flights by Berliner coalmen, not as tolerant, resourceful nor humorous as the piano movers, but then their money wasn't so good. Boden are German attics divided up into individual kingdoms by wooden partitions. Ours, in the Victoriastrasse, was hellishly cold. We kept our coal in an old bath which had somehow strayed there; odd because there were no bathrooms, as far as I know, in the whole massive building. There was also a flat roof to which we had access. It had a fine view of the Potsdammerstrasse, the Potsdammerplatz, the Wilhelmstrasse and beyond that the tops of the trees in the Tiergarten.

The first night we moved in we stoked up the iron stove in the studio till it glowed red hot all night. It was a very cold winter and at one moment I burned my pictures as there was a coal shortage. I hadn't got used to the cold temperatures and couldn't bear to go out. To see the prostitutes standing there in minus 30 degrees in their thin shoes and stockings was ghastly.

I went to Poland to paint my paysage.[1] I arrived in Krakow on a beautiful June morning having travelled overnight from Berlin, and innocently asked in German for a room in a hotel. I didn't get one as Germans were not popular in Poland and single German females didn't get rooms in hotels. I walked into the market place which was a blaze of colour, flowers and fruit and Polish peasants in national costume, really lovely. By chance I met a Paris acquaintance who gave me a room in his flat. He had a lovely flat in an old palace just off the main square. There were a lot of rumours about this man. He was married to a Russian princess, but it was said that he had another wife in England and that he had been deported from England. I half hoped he would seduce me. Some of our Polish friends said that he was half-Jewish and half-German and they held this against him. There was a lot of anti-semitism in Poland. He was very kind to me. Apart from giving me a room, for which I meanly didn't pay, he took me to the artists' café in Krakow and introduced me to the artists Pronasco, Kowalski, Zibulski, Tomorovitch and Smorski.

There is a tower in the main square in Krakow from which every hour a trumpeter blows a call; one of the most beautiful things in the world. Chlapowski's brother, the pianist, turned up and I got a room with an

1 landscape

old aunt of his. It wasn't nearly so nice, but with a ridiculous sense of propriety, I thought it more suitable. In those days there was still a proper ghetto in Krakow where the Jews went about with their black caps and ringlets.

Tomorovitch, Smorski and I went to a village to paint paysage. We stayed in the village inn owned by Jews. It was also the village shop, so that the economic life of the village was in their hands, and I think this was the pattern in a great many Polish villages. We stayed there about a fortnight. It wasn't a very successful expedition because as usual I fell in love; with Tomorovitch. This was a dead loss, but I did do one rather nice water colour, and learned something about Polish villages. I took the train by myself to Zakopane. I stayed at a small village pension and it rained. In those days Zakopane was a small village mountain resort, but it had quite a lot of restaurants and cafes, one with a cabaret. It was there that I first heard the song "I kiss your little hand" which became so popular all over Europe. The weather improved. Mary, my sister, arrived along with Smorski and Kowalski from Krakow and a party of English students. Among the latter was a Nancy Samuel and this brought about a rather a comical situation because our Polish artists, with the exception of Pronaski and Smorski, were pretty much anti-semites. Nancy, sophisticated and charming, and daughter of a lord, had none of the fears and inhibitions of most Polish Jews. She made no secret of her Jewishness and would not eat pork.

Mary, Smorski, Kowalski and I went for a walking tour in the high Tatra. Smorski brought his girl friend. We went up the mountain as far as we could in a bus and then started walking. It became very misty and we became lost, but in the end at about 9 o'clock at night, we found our way down the mountainside to the youth hostel. Mary and I were fairly well equipped as she had proper climbing boots and I had a pair of hand-made Polish shoes which were very good. Smorski's girl friend had high heels, one of which broke climbing down the mountain in the dark, but she never gave in. She and Kowalski had to go back, but Mary, Smorski and I went on for a few more days until our money ran out. In the end we had only dry bread to eat and were attacked by a fierce dog. Smorski very bravely tried the trick of looking at it upside down between his legs. It worked. Later he was killed in the war serving in the resistance. The Polish hostels were very nice and clean. Everybody, men and women, slept in one big dormitory. We went back to Krakow and stayed a few more days. Mary went back to Berlin. I had a visit in my hotel room from Gottlieb, a Jewish artist. I wanted to show him some of the water colours that I had painted. They were in an ancient holdall that I had left with Chlapowski's aunt. I opened it and a stream of black beetles poured from it and as quickly disappeared into the room, like magic. Gottlieb went as white as a sheet and disappeared out of the door almost as quickly. A Jew introducing black beetles into a Polish hotel might have had some unpleasant consequences. I just stood there, petrified. There wasn't anything I could do about it and I thought, under the circumstances, there wasn't much point in confessing my crime to the management.

I got back to Berlin to find our studio in the Victoria Strasse beautifully clean. Yussef and a German architect called Heinrich Schaeffer had even succeeded in having the windows cleaned. Schaeffer wanted to marry me. One night I went with him to a carnival ball. I thought I had lost my key so I went home with him, and slept with him. Afterwards I felt tremendously good, although I was completely frigid. I enjoyed getting a man worked up. When I got home I found I had my key all the time. I suppose I just wanted to do that.

Our communist friend Peter Peri[1] had a studio in the Potsdammer Strasse that was right at the top of the house. As there were no door bells, we whistled a bar of the Marseillaise, and if he was there, he shouted down. Peri's house was being rebuilt and he had to get out. He was given compensation so we clubbed together and took two flats in a modern block in Templehof. By this time anyone who had money could get a flat as half of the new blocks stood empty. The unemployed were beginning to move out into the Laubenkolonie;[2] building shacks out of old packing cases, corrugated iron and tar paper. We paid the premium with Peri's compensation and our long suffering parents lent us the rest. One had to put down a premium that was returned when we moved in. We had a door made through the wall so that it was one big apartment. We had two big rooms: one of which I used as my studio and the other was Peri's. Of the two smaller rooms, one was used as our dining room and the other became Mary's piano room. One of the two kitchens Peri used as a workshop. Last but not least we had two bathrooms with run-

1 Also known as Laszlo Peri, 1899-1967, sculptor and painter

2 allotments

ning hot water and central heating. Since leaving home we had never had a bathroom so, on moving in, we spent the first evening luxuriating: having baths and showers.

We started, under Peri's influence, to read Marx, and to me it made sense, and still does. On 1st May 1930 the Mayday march was not forbidden. We joined it and marched all the way to Neukölln. We joined the Communist Party; there was branch in Tempelhof. In our block of flats there were three students from the Bauhaus, also Communist Party members: Ernst, Etel and Willi. Ernst and Etel were married and Willi lived with them. Willi had studied photography at the Bauhaus and was trying to get work as a freelance reporter. I had also taken up photography; painting seemed a bit pointless.

Peri knew Frau Moholy, who had a school for photography in Berlin, and I went there.[1] I borrowed thirty pounds from my parents and bought a Makina reflex camera. It had a good lens but was a difficult lens to hold. When one took a photograph the mirror jumped automatically and this tended to jar the camera. I was a bad photographer because I'm long-sighted and couldn't really see to focus properly. It took me ages to understand why.

Frau Moholy was also a Bauhaus person. We knew about the Bauhaus because Yussef had once taken us there to a dance. We stayed the night, sleeping in the washroom, wrapped up in our fur coats. Mine was a very splendid one bought by Yussef in Berlin: Russian pitchinuke, a real beauty. That time we walked by the Elbe; it was winter. Willi and I started living together and I became pregnant. Mary was pregnant too. I didn't want a baby then and had an abortion. It was very easy in those days. I went to a nursing home and stayed there five days. It made me very depressed. Mary wanted her baby and kept it.

My parents came to Berlin to see us. I think they were worried about what sort of life we were living. They stayed in a hotel in the Potsdammerplatz. The first day they arrived, Mary took mother and told her that she was having a baby and was going to marry Peter Peri. They accepted the situation. Peter and Mary couldn't get married until Peter got his divorce. Our parents came out to the apartment in Tempelhof. We discretely covered the door which joined the two flats with a wall hanging, and didn't divulge the true position. They met Willi, who they

1 Lucia Moholy 1894–1989, photographer

didn't like. They said he was a miserable specimen, small and skinny.

We decided to go to London and try to do photo reportage for the A.I.Z.[1] This was an illustrated newspaper run by Willi Münzenberg, rather like Picture Post. I think the latter was probably inspired by German picture papers such as Berliner Illustrierte and others.

So we started off for England; we went to Hamburg by the night train. We had a friend in Hamburg, Steven Humphries Owen. He was rich and had a car. We went around the shipping agents looking for a ship to take us to England. I had a very unpleasant experience with a paternoster. These were moving lifts that circulated all the time. You had to step into them when they came level with the floor. I got into one too quickly and fell two feet or so, twisting my foot. Steven took us for a ride around Hamburg and gave us tea. We found a ship that was going to Hull that night. We arrived in London the next day, the 1st August, and stayed with my younger sister Anne in her flat in Chelsea. She took us out to lunch in a pub in the King's Road and gave us beer and ham sandwiches. I thought it was lovely. We sat outside in the pale hazy London sunshine. Anne was going to Ireland for the family tribal ritual holiday and she lent us her flat.[2] I was introduced to the English sink and that deeply individual smell of Jeyes Fluid and dampness; English gas with its splendid flames and tremendous hiss. Being middle class, I had never been allowed into an English kitchen, and in Ireland where we were allowed into the kitchen, the stove was a coal one. Continental gas rings were miserable things compared. In Anne's flat, which was on the ground floor, the bath was in the kitchen under the kitchen table. It had a geyser, so one had to open the window when having a bath, for fear of being asphyxiated.

I joined the Communist Party. Willi didn't because we were afraid he might be deported. We were very conspiratorial about our actions. This was partly romanticism on our part but it did have a basis of reality.

In those days the West London branch of the Communist Party had rooms in the Fulham Road. The secretary was Humphrey Slater.[3] He had been at the Slade Art School the same time as me. He suggested to us that we go up to Cumberland and do reportage of the miners' strike

1 Arbeiter Illustrierte Zeitung

2 Biddy's parents owned a seaside house in Portballintrae in N.Ireland. Aunts, uncles, cousins and their friends congregated there for the summer holidays.

3 1906-1958 British author and painter. He fought in the Spanish Civil war.

in Whitehaven. I pawned my Berlin fur coat for five pounds, and we went by coach up the Great North Road through the night. We stayed a night in Keswick, pretending to the landlady that we were married. We were very nervous about this, but the landlady didn't seem interested and gave us a very good tea with bacon and eggs. The next day we took a bus down to Workington to see Hymie Lee who was the party organiser. He wasn't in; we were told he was at a meeting in Whitehaven, so we went there and took some photographs of the meeting. There was a march after the meeting, but we were afraid that if Willi was caught by the police photographing the demonstration, he would be deported. Hymie Lee told us to go and wait for him at the home of one of the strike leaders. We reached the house at about four o'clock in the afternoon. Only the children were there, everybody else was at the demonstration. They had no shilling for the gas and I was too shy to produce one. We sat in the dark till the people came back at eleven o'clock at night. I was terribly shy, very conscious of class, and thought of myself as a member of 'society'. I didn't know how to behave with 'working men'. Hymie Lee took us to a pub. I didn't know how to behave in a pub as I'd never been in one, except on that first day with Anne in the King's Road. We went to the strike canteen organised by the miner's wives; it was brilliantly organised. The feeling of people getting together to do something for an idea; I had never experienced anything like it. Our lives seemed to be one unending status grab; everybody just grasping for themselves. We went back by bus to Keswick and then to Liverpool. From there we took the night bus to London to get our photographs developed. They were good. The Daily Worker took some and so did the A.I.Z. in Germany. My period came and I was feeling ill from the bus trip.

Anne was coming home from Ireland so we had to find somewhere else to live. We found a furnished flat on the top floor of 211 Fulham Road just on the corner of Redcliffe Gardens where the 31 bus goes. We saw a rather sordid pair of empty rooms with a wonderful view of the Lots Road power station, but settled for the less romantic and more comfortable. We had a view of the Express Dairy shop opposite and we could watch and hear the coalmen pass with their great carthorses. We had a tom cat that we had met one night as we were coming home and he stayed with us for a while. Willi and the cat used to catch mice together. The mice hid in the gas stove which stood on the landing. Willi would suddenly open the door and the cat would pounce. It was rather a cruel sport and I didn't really approve, but the mice were a nuisance. The people on the floor below also had a tom cat and the two of them would sit on the stairs making faces at each other. They never actually fought.

Willi went to the British Museum. He had a ticket for the reading room and he read Karl Marx. Of course this was rather ridiculous, and a measure of our innocence and romanticism. It was homage to Marx. Willi would have done better to have learned English instead of mystically reading Marx in the British museum.

Our next effort was South Wales. It was the Invergordon time.[1] The Worker's Theatre Movement did a sketch and I played the part of the sailor who led the revolt. The actual sailor helped us to produce it. We rehearsed one week in the cellar of the Daily Worker in Tabernacle Street and then went off to South Wales in Tom Thomas's van. Willi came with us to do the photographs. It was rather a splendid drive, starting at Shepherds Bush, which still had the little houses round the green where now there are big office blocks. We went through the New Forest[2] singing the Russian song about the five year plan. I argued about the translation, which did sound awfully silly:

'Five year plan of socialist construction, we'll complete, we'll complete, complete the five year plan in four.'

We stayed the night in Cardiff in an extraordinary bug ridden ancient hostel; it can't have changed much since Fielding's time, and went on to Tonypandy, where we were given hospitality in miners' homes. We played our sketches to packed enthusiastic halls. We were pretty awful, didn't know our lines and had to be prompted all the time. Only one of the sketches was any good; it was about the prisoners in Meerut[3] in India. We had bars which we held up and then each of us said a bit. Of course this was 1931 with ghastly unemployment and the means test. The enthusiasm of the Welsh miners for the Russian revolution was tremendous.

In the early morning we used to hear the miners going to work up the steep streets. Once there was an alarm due to an accident in the mine.

1 Invergordon Mutiny 1931. British Government announced salary cuts for Government employees, this included seamen's pay. Industrial action taken by 1000 sailors of British Atlantic Fleet.

2 Forest of Dean?

3 1929. Trade Unionists, including three Englishmen, were arrested for organising a railstrike.

The whole town streamed to the pit head and we all stood there. Fortunately nobody had been badly hurt. From there we went to Bristol by train. The hunger march was on its way and we brought the news to a meeting on the downs where Harry Pollit was speaking.[4] In Bristol we stayed with a photographer. He developed our photographs for us in the room in which he lived, which was a cellar. He did it by candlelight; developed the film; didn't wash it, and put it straight into the fixing bath by full candlelight. Willi, trained at the Bauhaus to absolute hygienic cleanliness, watched in horror this method, but the result was the most perfect negative we ever had.

We came back with the hunger marchers who were marching to London: all men from the valleys led by Wall Hannington. We left them on the windy roads that Lear and Gloucester and the Romans must have passed, and took the train to London to get our photographs to the Daily Worker.

The hunger march arrived in London, and there were some very tough demonstrations around the Houses of Parliament. Some demonstrators rolled marbles under the horses of the Cossacks as the mounted police were called. It was while photographing these demonstrations that we came to grief. It happened like this. The demonstrations were in the evening and one had to use flash light. In those prehistoric days we did it with a little heap of magnesium powder piled onto a little tin tray which had a handle and a contraption like a cigarette lighter with a flint. One held the camera in one hand and the tin tray in the other; pressed both knobs and prayed. Sometimes it worked with Willi, never with me. The powder had only to get slightly damp, which on a drizzly November day was extremely likely. On this fateful demonstration we saw the press photographers had a marvellous new invention: an electric light that was automatically linked to the camera and flashed reliably at the right second. Willi, who was a technical enthusiast, went up to the press photographers who kindly explained it to us and told us where we could purchase it: the civil servants store in Victoria Street. About five minutes later we found ourselves surrounded by three seemingly large detectives. I am five feet four and Willi was about the same. They didn't actually do anything very terrible; just questioned us about Willi's permit to stay in

4 1890-1960 Head of Trade Union dept. and then General Secretary of British Communist Party.

England. We went home very sober and spent half the night burning our copies of Imprecor: a perfectly legal monthly journal of the Comintern. Nothing much happened really; we had two visits from the police, the second of which was from much nastier officers. I always regretted wasting a cigarette on one of them. They asked us if we could speak Russian to which we truthfully replied that we couldn't. Willi couldn't even speak English; however it put the wind up us and we thought it would be better not to try to prolong Willi's permit which was only for six months.

We became even more conspiratorial, and when the West London Branch of the Communist Party went to visit a Russian ship that was lying in the Pool of London, Willi wasn't allowed to come. We visited the ship full of our romance about Russia. We wanted to see the Lenin corner and the men's quarters. The captain wanted to show us the beautiful inlaid woodwork in the first-class saloon. I was a little jolted by the Lenin corner, done in red velveteen with a very hoarse gramophone pouring out turgid music. The captain was very nice but I think he thought we were entirely barmy.

We had another problem; we weren't married and my parents didn't know we were living together in the flat in the Fulham road. The fiction was that I was staying with Anne. If my mother phoned, Anne would say that I was having a bath, then she would ring me in the Fulham Road and I would ring my mother back. The point was that our main source of income was my allowance. It became too obvious, and we were summoned to appear at my parent's house in Sheffield Terrace.

We had a very unfortunate interview. My mother was very angry. When she was angry her neck went bright red, and like all angry people she looked ridiculous. Willi's sense of humour came out always at tactless moments; he couldn't help laughing and when he laughed he had a grin that went from ear to ear, most irritating for the incensed parent. They made us promise not to see each other for six months and not to write. We suggested marriage, but this didn't go down at all well, as I was twenty six and Willi was three years younger. It was absurd. We gave the promise without the slightest intention of keeping it. At that time it was practically impossible to get a job. We felt that they had no moral right to enforce terms on us, however the net result of all this was that we decided we had better leave England. We wanted to go to Russia. The Daily Worker and Russia Today, the monthly journal of the British Soviet Society, thought it was a good idea. They weren't getting good photographs from Russia and we thought we could do some better ones. So we packed Willi's mitgard lamp and our Leica enlarging machine. We left behind: the beautiful oak table which Steven had given us and which we had to saw in half to get into the flat; a beautiful piece of Russian material bought at Derry and Toms which we used as a bedcover which Willi didn't like; an oil picture by me painted from the top of the Sheffield Terrace house of the dawn over Notting Hill Gate; and a very nice print of London. Anne salvaged the table and the print. I was heavy hearted as I was beginning to love my native land.

We went back to Berlin. Mary and Peter had got married and they had moved from Tempelhof to Siemanstadt. They had a lovely flat on the ground floor with grass and oak trees in front of it. The flats were designed by Gropius from the Bauhaus. Mary was expecting her baby in February. We stayed with them. We went to see the British liaison man from the Comintern in Berlin, but he wasn't able to help us much with our Russian plan. The difficulty was that we didn't have enough money. We had just enough to buy photo material and pay the journey and then we would have been flat broke. We wanted some sort of guarantee that we would be able to earn something when we got there, but there was no question of this, so we gave it up, rather sadly. Berlin was already beginning to give me the creeps.

We had to find somewhere to live before Mary's baby arrived. A friend of Peter's, Ursel Demle, had a house in Schmargendorf. She let us a room on the top floor. There was no central heating but we had a good stove. Ursel had been married to the poet Demle. She was very young when she married and she wanted to have babies. She had two little girls and they lived out in the country. Her marriage broke up so she got a divorce, came to Berlin and married again. Her second husband, Will, had been in prison. At the end of the war in 1919 he became mixed up with a band of hooligans. They robbed an old woman who owned a shop and killed her. Will was standing guard outside and had nothing to do with the murder. He was the only one to be caught and was given a life sentence. His case was taken up in the Reichstag and after seven years in prison he was pardoned. It made him terribly bitter and difficult to get on with. Ursel's relations took her children away.

Mary had her baby, a girl called Ann. She had it in the same nursing home that I had my abortion. She was the only one having a baby there; everybody else was having an abortion. I became pregnant again, but we didn't want to settle down, so I had another abortion. This time I didn't go to the nursing home; the doctor did it with an anaesthetic and I came home in a taxi. I was perfectly all right but it made me terribly depressed.

Will was also a photographer. He and Ursel bought a motorbike and were going to Spain to do reportage for the Berliner Illustrierte. They asked Willi to go with them. We put up a third of the money and they went on the motorbike with a sidecar. I was to stay on in the house and collect the rent from the other lodgers and pay it. I joined the Rote Sprachrohr. This was an agitprop group, a theatre group doing political sketches. Mary was their pianist. I think she was very good. When she left, Max the producer, wanted me to play the piano for them, but as I couldn't play, I was in the chorus. I had a good voice. I couldn't do speaking parts because my German wasn't good enough. There is a saying, I believe it was the English composer Holst who said it, "If a thing is worth doing, it's worth doing badly". Certainly our English group subscribed to it, and I personally think there is a lot in it, but the Germans aren't like that. We used to rehearse every evening and we had practically only one programme which the troupe had been doing for years. It was called the U.S.S.R. programme. It was a constructivist piece illustrating the Russian revolution. We were rehearsed until we were really brilliant and the show was first class. We used to perform two or three times a week, going out to small towns and villages around Berlin, and also in the various districts of Berlin. I grew terribly frustrated. I hated the discipline and took to reading Edgar Wallace detective stories.

Humphrey Slater came to Berlin. He'd been to Russia and he said Moscow was rather like Berlin. He wanted to learn German. He stayed with Witvogel, who was a communist political writer. I went to see him there and he came to visit us in Siemanstadt. His wife Elizabeth wanted a divorce, and he wanted me to help him give her evidence for it, but I wouldn't. I thought it hard on my father who was a judge. My sister Anne had already figured in the divorce courts and I thought two daughters were a bit much. We had a painful affair. He came one night to Schmagendorf; it was a miserable business. I really wanted an excuse to go back to England. He was my countryman and he was good looking and his mind was tremendously alive and stimulated me intellectually, which Willi didn't. He went back to England. I only saw him once again.

There seemed nothing for it but to stick it out in Germany. I had left the Rote Sprachrohr. Willi was coming back from Spain and I felt I couldn't let him down. They came back at the end of August. Willi was burned a sort of purple by the Spanish sun. Will and he had got to the point where they couldn't get on at all. Will wanted Willi to make prints of the negatives he had done, but as they were in debt to the photo agents, there was no chance of us getting any money so we gave him the negatives.

It was September 1932. We moved to Reinickendorf to a new estate called Weissenstadt. The houses were painted white, centrally-heated, with two tall chimneys in the middle. Most of the flats were empty. All around were the Lauben kolonie, allotments with huts built out of bits of wood, tar paper and tea chests, where the unemployed lived. Our flat was in the bridge house, built on stilts over the road, five stories high. It had three rooms: a kitchen alcove, a bath and lavatory, and a big balcony. We were on the second floor. Friends from the Bauhaus lived next door; we were all in the communist party. We had no furniture but a comrade, Mrs Fritches, gave us a table and we made a bed, or rather a frame, and bought a mattress. Ursel gave us some tea cloths, linen ones, which was very nice of her considering we had the row with them. I'm thankful to say they both survived the war. I made some little red curtains for the kitchen window. When I came home late, it was marvellous to see them lighted up and to know that Willi was there. We both had bicycles.

There was the tram strike, which the Berlin Nazis supported. Willi did some photographs of a meeting at the tram depot in Reinickendorf. We also went out at night with the idea of taking up tramlines. The Nazis did this too but they were much better at it. The strike collapsed. In November there were elections. We had a banner, which we stretched from our balcony to the Gebhard's as they had a flat further along the corridor. One night the Nazis tried to haul it down. They threw up some sort of grappling iron, but Willi was very extremely brave and crawled out onto the balcony and disentangled it. Gebhard kept turning the stair light on so that the Nazis would think there were a lot of us. Fortunately they didn't come up to see.

The communists held an election meeting in a hall in Reinickendorf to which the Nazis came. We were inside the meeting and we could hear them singing. It was very frightening. They broke all the windows but nobody was hurt. The police came in time so they didn't come into the hall. After that it was impossible for the Communist Party to get a hall.

At Christmas time Willi and I went for a skiing holiday in the Riesenbirge. We stayed in a peasant house. The whole family in the winter time lived and slept in one room. The beds were round the wall, two-tiered, with red and white checked bed covers. There was a wooden churn in the room. It worked on a lever attached to the ceiling; all hand carved. I think that living room must have looked almost exactly the same in the seventeenth century. It was a lovely holiday, although we had too much snow for good skiing.

We came back to the dirt and the horridness of Berlin in time for the Lenin Liebknecht and Luxemburg demonstration on 12th January 1933. I carried a banner all the way from Karl Liebknecht Haus to the cemetery, where Liebknecht and Luxemburg are buried.[1] There was twelve degrees of frost and I had a bad turn of lumbago as a result; the first time that I'd ever had it.

1 Karl Liebknecht and Rosa Luxemburg, 1871-1919 Leaders of German revolution that helped to end W.W.1. They were captured and murdered.

Chapter 2 1933–1939

Then came the 30th January 1933; Hitler, Reichskanzler. We watched the swastika flags coming out in the Weissenstadt. They looked rather pretty against the white houses. It was a brilliant frosty day. That night we were wandering about to see if anything was happening. Coming home at about one o'clock in the morning along the Berlinerstrasse we saw a comrade standing on the street giving out leaflets. They were small, drawn in pencil, with a neat little pattern around the edge, and on them was written, 'All out for a political general strike'. It seemed absolutely futile, although very brave. We looked at this pathetic scrap of paper, gave it back to him and told him to give it to somebody else as we were communists any way. We went home.

In the Communist Party branch of Weissenstadt, Herr Sachs and his wife who were Jewish were hauled out in the middle of the night. They let her go after a few weeks but he died in a concentration camp. A boy, a student called Fritches, was arrested but he too was let out. Later, another man, I can't remember his name, was taken to S.A.[1] house in Pankow. They beat him up and shaved off half his hair. His wife was in a terrible state. Hans, from the allotments, was held at the police station and made to lie in a coffin but his cousin who, was a policeman, rescued him. Nothing happened to us. Most of the Communist Party members in Weissenstadt moved away. Charlie, a medical student, went to his family in Hanover. His wife was Hungarian Jewish. They got a divorce, otherwise he would not have been able to continue his studies. On the top floor there was a writer, Heinz Neukranz. He and his wife were arrested. She got out later and went to Czechoslovakia. We alone stayed on for a while. Then Mary in Siemanstadt was arrested. She and Peri had a lot of communist literature. They couldn't burn it as they had no stove so Mary loaded it all onto the pram and took it to the comrades in the allotments. She walked straight into the Gestapo who took her to the Alexanderplatz police station. Peri went and protested. He still had Hungarian nationality and he got her out. They went to England in a hurry, leaving all their furniture in the flat in Siemanstadt. In the end we

1 Sturmabteilung, brown shirts

Biddy, Mary (Biddy's older sister) and Peter Peri in a Berlin flat taken in 1930s

were evicted out of the Weissenstadt flat. There had been a rent strike and we owed rent. We let ourselves be evicted. It was a peaceful affair. The bailiff arrived with a cart; we loaded our belongings onto it and drove through the Jungfernheide forest, by the canal, to Siemenstadt. We moved into Mary and Peri's flat.

We decided to get married. Of course we didn't think Hitler would last, and if we were going to work illegally in the German Communist Party, it was better to conform outwardly. But there were deeper reasons. My whole upbringing had stressed the importance of being married and getting the status of a married woman. Also, I wanted to break my dependence on my sister and this was a very radical way of doing it. I didn't consciously accept these reasons but rationalised the whole thing as my part in the revolutionary struggle against fascism. We put up the banns in Siemanstadt and I wrote to my parents. They wrote back forbidding me to marry Willi and insisting I come home first. This I wouldn't do. I was afraid if once I left Germany, I wouldn't have the pluck to return; I felt that I must carry on and do what I intended. My parents cut off my allowance, leaving us with no financial basis. This really did the trick as far as I was concerned. An unearned income is an excellent thing, but if it means you cannot make your own decisions on such important things as whether you marry or not, and where you live. It is not worth it. So we were married in Siemanstadt registry office. Gert Schneider and Friedel Kopitch from the Weissenstadt were our witnesses. For our wedding breakfast we had goulash and rhubarb which I cooked myself. No drinks as we didn't have the money for it.

We pawned our cameras. Willi had no money sense. He decided that he needed a new pullover. We were going out to see Gert and Hank Schneider on our bicycles. I suppose it was about ten miles and we had to go through the centre of Berlin. Willi bought himself a pullover for fifteen marks. Our whole worldly wealth consisted of about forty marks. You could get pullovers for five marks. When he came out of the shop, proudly with his purchase, I was aghast and furious and told him to go back and change it for a cheap one. Willi just laughed and cycled off. He could cycle much faster than I could. I followed him the ten miles weeping with rage. However in the end I saw the funny side of it. After all, whether you have forty or twenty five marks between you and destitution doesn't make much difference and it was a nice pullover. He always wanted to buy things when we were at our last gasp in the way of cash.

When we were fairly flush and I said, "If you want to buy something, now's the time", he never wanted anything. Actually about a week later my sister sent us three pounds. We lived on potato and bean soup, scraps of bacon rind that you could get cheap, bread and margarine and ersatz coffee. Buske and Gebhard were in the same predicament, although they did get the dole. We didn't because we weren't registered and had been working freelance.

The spring came. We used to go out to the lakes on our bicycles and bathe. All the time there were ghastly stories of people being arrested, beaten up, even murdered. We were very panicky. We did get one or two illegal news letters. I read them sitting on the lavatory, ready to flush them down if there was a ring on the bell

I went to the British embassy and had my passport cancelled. I was allowed to keep it as a souvenir; it came in very handy later. I felt terribly depressed at giving up my British citizenship. Mary and Peri had arrived safely in England. Mary got busy on the family and organised aunts and uncles, so that about June my parents caved in and I received my allowance again. In fact this allowance was in my name because it was one of the ways of avoiding income tax. They had no right to cut it off and I could have gone to the law about it, and indeed I would have done. We gave some money to Gebhard and Buske, bought ourselves a little pop-pop motorcycle and left Berlin. We rode through the sandy soil and pine forests of the Mark to Magdeburg, on through the rich rolling farm country to the Rhine. We imagined that in the Ruhr, the heart of German industry, the workers would be stirring; if only we could get contact. We reached Düsseldorf on the 3rd May. We stayed for a night or two in a little inn near the centre of town. We had a nasty experience coming out of the cinema one evening. I was smoking a cigarette, and some brown shirts followed us shouting rude remarks as they thought we were French. Actually Willi did look rather French, however when they realised I was British they left us in peace. We found a flat in a housing estate in the industrial part of town, Benzstrasse 11 where a half the houses stood empty. The unemployed lived in the Lauben kolonie allotments stretching around the town. Our rent was thirty-five marks a month. There was neither heating nor gas stove although there was a gas main in the house. We had to buy all these things ourselves. We bought an electric fire, but never having had electric fires before, we thought it would be enough. We also bought a double gas ring. Of course the electric fire couldn't cope with the German winter, so we bought a lovely round second-hand stove. It had rings on the top so you could cook on it. We had three rooms and a lavatory but no bathroom.

There were six flats in the house, two were empty. One of our neighbours was Herr Stephanie, a catholic, who was in the S.A.[1] He had five children, dear little boys who were thrilled with Willi, his motorcycle and camera. At the top lived Herr Reck, a baker by trade. He had three children. Frau Reck was very like a Londoner, she did a bit of charring sometimes. Herr Reck was not in the S.A. Then there were the Schulzes who were older and had no children. He really was a Nazi. Everybody was unemployed. We used to spend most evenings with the Recks who had a lovely warm kitchen with a Dutch oven which stood on legs. They had a wireless, a Volks Emphanger. We listened to the reports of the Reichstag trial. None of us ever actually made a comment, just occasionally an indirect remark, but we could tell and they could tell, and we knew that they knew, we weren't Nazis and neither were they. They probably knew that we were communist and they probably had been too, at least communist voters. But of course everybody was very careful. Their only comment on the programme came when there was classical music. They would turn it off in disgust and say "Symphony". Frau Schulz, apart from being a Nazi was a horrid snob. She had a washing machine in her cellar, a wooden barrel on legs that you turned with a handle. She wouldn't lend it to Frau Reck or Frau Stephanie, but she offered it to me. I discussed with the others whether I should accept the offer. They said I should, so I did and it did save a lot of scrubbing. In Bremen my mother-in-law had a washing machine, a Wasserdruck machine. You turned the cold water tap on and the pressure of it worked the machine. The only snag was that a lot of water leaked. They had it in an outhouse in the yard; I believe they've still got it. Actually the Nazis seemed more aggressive in Düsseldorf than they had been in Berlin. I think this was because of the French occupation after the First World War. One day a Nazi parade was going along the main street. They forced everybody to do Heil Hitler but my husband wouldn't and managed to get out of the way in time. They came round one Sunday morning with a weekly illustrated paper called the Brauner Post. They forced their way into thc flats. The whole house took out a subscription; there was obviously no choice if you didn't want to get beaten up. We only paid for the first week and as they didn't come again, everybody dropped it, including the Schulzes. They preferred the Morganpost which was a little in the style of the Daily Mirror. It had a good serial and for a German paper, not much political news, just murders and little snappy items about illnesses. Some friends from Berlin visited us. They had got married in spite of the fact that the wife was Jewish. At the beginning, one could get married without producing a pedigree as I didn't have to either. She was pregnant. They were hitch hiking through Germany selling picture postcards and begging. They stayed with us for about three weeks and then went on their way. She was a hunchback and he was a feckless individual. Afterwards, she had the baby but he abandoned her. She came to see me later in Berlin with her little boy. It was just at the time when we thought we were going to do some really vital illegal work for the Communist Party, so I didn't encourage her to come again. I gave her some rather nasty marrow jam I had made, and I remember looking down from our balcony in the Gubitzstrasse, seeing her pushing her push chair with the baby in it and the big jar of marrow jam. That was the last I saw of her.

I went to England twice from Düsseldorf as it wasn't such a long way. The first time I went, I was horrified to find myself obviously on the black list. Having a German passport, I had to go through immigration, and when it came to my turn, the officer went away and seemed to be looking me up. He came back and questioned me. It took much longer than anybody else. On all these journeys there were Jews in an awful state of anxiety. I felt terribly sorry for them. First they had the boat journey and probably felt sea sick, then immigration, and the ones that were turned back had the crossing again. It must have been ghastly, because even I felt nervous and I didn't really have much to worry about, being born British and being on a visit to my family. The most hair-raising occasion was when I came on the ship 'Bremen' after Clara was born. She was ten months old and I had left her with my mother-in-law. The immigration officers came onto the ship and did it in the first class lounge. The chap let me through, and as I was walking to the gangway, called me back. I had to wait with all the German officials looking on until every one else was finished. Then he asked me in a very loud voice if my husband was a communist. He let me through in the end, and I found afterwards that they had broken the lock of my suitcase. I don't know if the German officials heard what he said, they certainly could see that something was wrong. Nothing happened when I returned to

Germany. It was on this same trip that the 'Bremen' ran into a great anti-fascist demonstration on reaching New York. This may have put everything else out of the mind of the 'Bremen' officers.

We moved to Hamburg. Willi's family lived in Bremen. We found a flat in Wandsbeck on the fourth floor of a small block. It had central heating, a bathroom and two long rooms with parquet floors. The hochbahn ran not far away and we could hear the trains rumbling along. This was homely for me; all my life I had heard the sound of trains. We decided to have a baby and I became pregnant at the first try. Being pregnant made me rather more homesick than I already was, but still the idea of making a new life, a new person, was tremendously positive. Even in those dark days we had no doubts about the future. Atom bombs were as yet unknown. As a wedding present my brother gave us a wireless set. We bought a Dutch set with a short wave so that we could listen to Moscow. When the man came to install it, he showed us how it worked and said you'll find Moscow about there; Moscow wasn't marked on the chart. This set us in a flurry. He obviously wasn't trying to denounce us and at last we thought we were making contact. We invited him for supper and he bought along his boyfriend. It wasn't a very successful evening. I made whitebait and it wasn't very good. I'm a dead loss as a social hostess and it's only possible with a good deal of liquor. In those days we were too poor and too unsophisticated for drink. Actually, poor devil, I think he was half-Jewish and probably homosexual, so not the type to want to go in for revolutionary activity.

We listened to Moscow and the BBC. The BBC was much better value and a lot easier to get. Both were forbidden and if caught listening, you were sent to a concentration camp. It was pretty easy to avoid being caught and I don't think many people were. What happened was that they got caught telling other people what they had heard. I did get a conditioned reflex about turning down Big Ben and the peal of bells, which was the time signal for the BBC. Once in England on holiday, staying with my sister, I rushed to the wireless which was booming out "This is London" and turned it down before I realised what I was doing. Willi spent a good deal of time cleaning his motorbike which he had in a garage nearby. I really had nothing to do except clean the flat.

The spring came and we went on a visit to Berlin on the motorbike. We did it in one day. We stayed with Gebhard, Margaret and Buske. They were doing much better and had moved to the West End. They had a big flat in an old building in the Kantstrasse. It was decorated all white in modern style, very clean and light. They were doing commercial art. Margaret was very smart and good looking and was getting them the work. I went to see my old doctor who had done my abortions. She was very pleased that I wanted to have a baby, but she told me if I wanted to keep the pregnancy I'd better not ride on a motorbike because as far as she knew this was one of the best ways of getting rid of a baby. So I took the train back to Hamburg. It was a pleasant and comfortable journey in the new fast diesel train.

We had decided to move back to Berlin as we had our friends there and were much more likely to work for the party. We sold the bike, packed up and took the train to Berlin. We stayed again with Gebhard in the Kantstrasse while we looked for a flat. Gert Schneider, who was one of our witnesses when we were married, had a flat in the north of Berlin in the Gubitzstrasse. He too was married and had a job at the Soviet Embassy. His wife was the daughter of an important Austrian communist and she had worked as a nursemaid to one of the embassy staff. She got him the job. We visited them, found an empty flat in the same block and we took it. It was still fairly easy to get flats. Hitler's rearmament plan was only just beginning to get under way and mop up the unemployment. Our flat in the Gubitzstrasse was on the top floor. It had two big rooms overlooking the street, one with a balcony. The kitchen, bathroom and another small room were at the back. Sitting in the kitchen in the evenings, we could see the sun set behind the high old houses on the Prenzlauer Allee.

I was feeling much better. I was over my morning sickness, but was already beginning to look big; I have a back that curves in. Hanke, Gert's wife, had followed my example and was also pregnant. We both felt slightly superior; that smug self congratulary feeling that women get when having babies, as though they were doing something very clever and most commendable.

The house had eight flats, two on each floor: their front doors facing each other across the landing. Our neighbours, the Cornelsons, were Nazis. We knew this because on flagging days they hung out their swastika flag. They had a middle-size one and were always very punctual with it. In our house, out of the eight balconies, seven hung flags. Ours was the only one without.

There were different sorts of flags. The next floor down, under us, was a home made one. The other side, under the Cornelsons, a little one: the sort you buy at Epa[1] for one mark. Both these were very unpunctual and occasionally didn't come out at all. Beneath them were two big ones, and on the ground floor, again two big ones, but one of them tended not to come out. Another reason we knew the Cornelsons were Nazis was that he said "Heil Hitler" when he went to work in the mornings. Frau Cornelson would see him off at the door. He would say Heil Hitler and bound down the stairs and then she would wave to him from the balcony. In the evening the procedure was reversed. She would watch for him coming down the Gubitzstrasse and wave. He bounded up the stairs, Heil Hitler and in. He was an insurance clerk. They came from Hamburg. Poor soul, I think she was just as homesick for Hamburg as I was for England. All day long she was alone, cleaning her spotless flat, doing her shopping; she dressed rather dowdily with laced up shoes. I was fascinated by them. I wanted to know how their minds worked. I tried to get to know her. When she came out onto her balcony which adjoined ours, I would go out and say good morning. I did get to know her a bit. We both of us were very lonely really. When my baby was born, I asked her in to see it. She came across the landing into our flat and looked at Clara who lay in her cot.

'She's very small' was all she said.

Perhaps she thought that as we weren't Nazis we couldn't produce a rugged Germanic type. She had a baby herself later. It was a boy who they called it Peter. She had a very difficult birth and Peter couldn't suck, so Herr Cornelson had to suck out her breasts for her; it sounded horrid. We had one discussion about a case that was headlined in the newspapers. They of course took the Volkische Beobachter;[2] we took the Deutsche Allgemeine Zeitung. This case was about a woman who had abandoned her three children. The woman lived in a cellar flat near the Kottbuser Tor, a part of Berlin that is a bit like Soho. She was married to a man who was mentally deficient and who was in an institution, so that she was alone with the three children aged three, two and the youngest a few months old. She met a man in a café in the Kottbuserstrasse and went off with him. The neighbours didn't notice

1 German Woolworths

2 Newspaper of the German National Socialist party and official voice of the Nazi party

anything was wrong for about five days and when at last the police broke in, the two youngest children were dead and the eldest one died in hospital. The woman was found and condemned to death. A great deal was made of the story in the papers; the woman was made out as an example of wickedness. I said the welfare authorities were partly to blame; the woman having to cope on the dole in a cellar flat with three tiny children. Bringing up children wasn't just a matter of instinct; you needed intelligence and decent facilities. The filth and the poverty and the loneliness might have driven anybody to do it. After all she was only following the strongest instinct of all but Frau Cornelson didn't see it. We did have one or two discussions after, but it was risky.

Below the Cornelsons lived Oma,[1] she had the small Epa flag. I first became aware of her when I saw her standing one day in the hallway, leaning against the wall and muttering—

"I won't go to hospital, I won't go."

She didn't. I think she had something wrong with her bladder. I got to know her well. She lived with her adopted daughter Frau Stach, and Frau Stach's little boy, Arno. Frau Stach worked at the Femina nightclub in the Tauentzienstrasse in town. She came home very late in a taxi. She was very smart and very good looking. Oma came from the land, in Pomerania. She came to Berlin and worked in the market where she had a fruit stall. She took Frau Stach from the orphanage when she was seven. She was a very pretty little girl. Twice she had been adopted and twice sent back to the orphanage because she was so naughty, but Oma kept her and brought her up. When she was nineteen Arno was born; she wasn't married. Oma told the story of how they went to the hospital to have the baby, but when they got there Frau Stach didn't like it, so they went home again, called the doctor and Arno was born at home. As soon as he was born Oma gave him a bottle against the doctor's orders.

"I couldn't let him starve" she said, so he never took to the breast.

I think Arno's father was Jewish and I think he sent them some money. Arno used to come up and play with Clara. He was a dear little boy with dark curly hair. Oma used to come too, and we played snakes and ladders together. Oma used to tell stories of how she smuggled food in the First World War, bringing it in under her petticoats. When she was young the girls wore no knickers so if they wanted to piss they just stood

1 Grannie

still and let it go under their long skirts. When Queen Juliana of the Netherlands got married[1] she said,

"She's fat, but she'll get fatter."

She loved children and would have looked after Clara for me, but Clara was afraid of the great rugged old woman and her hoarse voice. But it all had a tragic ending. When Arno was ten, they wanted to send him to the Gymnasium[2]. He had to be tested to see if he was Jewish. I suppose Frau Stach wouldn't say who was the father. They measured Arno's head and took blood tests. They never told me what the result was but he never did go the Gymnasium. Then he became ill with leukaemia and got whiter and weaker until in the end he had to go to hospital. He was there for two months before he died. The two women went to visit him taking early strawberries and delicacies to tempt him, but he couldn't eat them. He had had so many blood transfusions that his body couldn't cope; his mouth was all sores. The night he died Oma came up to us. She was in a terrible state, so I went down and spent the night with her on the big double bed where the two women always slept together. She moaned all night. In the morning I telephoned the hospital for her. The sister told me that Arno was at peace and that Frau Stach was coming home. Oma knew what that meant. She pulled herself together and we cleaned the flat, first washing all the furniture, and then all the floors. When we had finished she seemed better, so I went upstairs. Then I heard Frau Stach coming home down the street screaming at the top of her voice. I could hear her coming up the stairs screaming and shouting. She went into the flat, the door shut and there was complete silence. I wondered if the two women had turned the gas on. I was too exhausted with the emotional strain to do anything about it. They hadn't. They had a very grand funeral, the coffin was open. I didn't go as I hate funerals. Oma threw herself into the grave and had to be dragged out. They moved away soon after. I met Frau Stach much later in the war. She told me that Oma was in the country living with farming people and that she was alright.

We did have a woman in the street who turned the gas on. She was a Nazi, a friend of Frau Cornelson. She had three children, one after another. When she found she was pregnant again, she killed herself.

1 Oma loved royalty

2 grammar school

Frau Cornelson was very shocked. She didn't believe in large families and Peter, as far as I know, remained an only child.

Underneath us lived the Zuhlkes who had the home made flag. They weren't Nazis. The reason for the homemade flag was economy. Herr Zuhlke was an engineering student and his wife helped him by selling cosmetics door to door. Afterwards he got a good job at Siemens. On the floor below them was Frau Rossade with her son and daughter. They were social democrats. She used to tell anti-Nazi jokes in the hallway but they put their big flag out just the same. Opposite them the tenants changed a lot. We had three different families during the time I lived there. Down at the bottom were an old couple who used to have a shop. They owned a rather nice dog and were definitely Hugenberg supporters[1] and Deutsch National.[2] Opposite them was an old woman with her son and daughter-in-law. They had been communists, but of course the flag went out, although occasionally it didn't. Flagging days were: 1st May, Hitler's birthday and one or two other days. It was four or five times a year and on special occasions, like the occupation of Austria and the re-militarising of the Rhineland.

June 30th 1934 was the day of the Roehm Putsch.[3] Hanka, Gert, Willi and I, sat on our balcony, enjoyed the summer sunshine and discussed the political situation. Hanka and Gert had moved out to a house with a garden in Hohenschönhausen. We used go there bicycling along the Frankfurter Allee.[4] It became very hot as the summer went on. I felt the heat badly, so we went for ten days to the Baltic. We stayed in a boarding house in a little seaside resort not far from Stettin. The weather turned cold and rainy but it did me the world of good. Mother had sent me some beautiful English woollen vests. It was lovely putting them on, so soft and white. She came to stay, and bought us a pram and a special wickelcommode: a sort of chest of drawers with a ledge around the top and a little mattress to dress the baby on. We bought them at Israel's, a big Jewish store which was still O.K. at the Alexander Platz. We bought a secondhand cot from friends. Mother lodged in a room we took for her

1 Rightwing politician 1861-1951, leading media proprietor, helped Hitler to power.
2 German National Peoples Party, a right wing party
3 Leaders of the S.A. arrested and shot
4 afterwards Stalin Allee

further down the Gubitzstrasse. I think she enjoyed being in Berlin. She could understand German quite well because when she was little they had Bavarian nurses, and she spoke German before she spoke English. Anyway like everybody else, it did her good to get away. I am a rotten housewife but I looked with pride and pleasure at the white painted cot, the wickelcommode and the pram, all new and clean for the baby. Mother went back to England. We saw her off at the station. She didn't have quite enough German currency, so we gave her ten marks, just in case she needed a cup of coffee on the train. When we got home about six o'clock and were sitting down to our supper, there was ring at the bell. The bell was always rather sinister if one didn't expect anybody; all the time we were rather afraid. Anyway I opened the door and on the landing stood the woman who cleaned the room mother stayed in. She held in her hand a three mark piece which she said that she had found. I explained that it was left her as a tip as mother had left without being able to see her and give it to her. She didn't seem quite to believe us. We reassured her and she went down stairs with the three mark piece in her hand, such a lot of money.

Klarchen, Willi's sister came to stay. We had a pleasant time going out to Wannsee and bathing. Klarchen was worried. She had been staying with her aunt in Stettin and it turned out that her uncle had syphilis and had infected his wife. Klarchen thought she had caught it. I tried to reassure her, saying that, as far as I knew, there was only one way of catching it. She went back to Bremen and of course, she was alright.

It was September 1934. We used to go out to the Tegelersee where some of the unemployed comrades from the Weissenstadt were living in a tent. We had to walk through the forest but Willi took his bike and wheeled me to the lake. I was very heavily pregnant and walking was a strain.

Towards the end of September the baby came. Klara Harprad came to see us. She was a teacher and had been a member of the party branch in the Weissenstadt. We didn't actually know her, so at first we were on our guard. She had dark bobbed hair, a rather intense face and was tall. She wanted us, or rather Willi, to do a job for the Party. This was to photograph a grave in Neueköln of a comrade who had been murdered and then make postcards to be used as propaganda material. Willi and another comrade went to the cemetery. They had a broad red ribbon with a slogan on it which they were to put on the grave and photograph.

When they arrived they found that there was a Nazi funeral going on but they decided to do it. They decorated the grave, took the photograph and then ran for it separately. Willi was followed but he fled into the allotments by the cemetery and escaped. That evening Buske came to see us. We didn't tell him about the photographs as we didn't quite trust him. Perhaps he sensed our mistrust, because we had a long argument about a film that was running in Berlin at that time; I can't remember what it was. Somehow hostility crept into the argument and he left. It had started to rain heavily and I watched him from our balcony sheltering down stairs in the hallway of our flats. We didn't call him back.

That night I started having labour pains but we waited until the following evening. Everybody said that if you went to the hospital too soon, they sent you home again I went to the Hedwigs hospital which was Catholic. In Berlin the Catholic hospitals were supposed to be the best while in the Rhineland it was the Evangelical hospitals. We got to the hospital about six o'clock and I was taken up in the lift. They examined me and said the opening was getting big enough. They gave me an enema and I was taken into the labour ward where there were three of us that night. I could see the other two women through gaps in the screens. One of them was old, about forty, she had a sallow face. It was her first baby and they knew it was dead. She had to go through the birth, and being a Catholic hospital, without any anaesthetic. A woman has to feel the pains of childbirth for the good of her soul. She kept asking for a rag soaked in vinegar, like Christ on the cross. The other was a young girl whose baby was illegitimate. She kept crying out wanting it to die. She had nowhere to live as her landlady wouldn't allow babies in the house. About three in the morning, the two doctors came over to me.

I heard them say "Let's get this one first."

They made my birth waters come and very quickly Clara was born. I could see her head with black hairs protruding from between my legs. Then she shot out on to the table and started to yell. I was deeply relieved as I was afraid my baby might be dead too. I kept asking the doctor: "Is it alive? Is it alive?"

The doctor washed her and brought her back to show me. "She's a beauty" he said.

She had a crumpled red face and black birth hairs growing all over her forehead. I kissed her forehead and welcomed her to the world before they took her away again. I felt wonderful but absolutely exhausted. They put a wide bandage around my tummy and an ice bottle on the top. They gave me a bell and told me to ring it if I was bleeding. After about an hour the porters came and I was wheeled along the corridor to the ward. The morning light was coming grey through the window. Over the house tops I could see a steeple with a clock on it. Birth is an extraordinary sensation. I thought at the time that it must be a little like dying. One feels that something is happening so basic: the life force that lies within one, moving in a primeval way. However, when the doctor said to me we'll see you again next year, I said I didn't want to go through that again.

Once in the ward, the nursing was very good. All the nurses were nuns. My bladder got stuck; sister gave me herb tea to drink but it didn't work and she had to use a catheter. After that it was O.K. Willi came but he was very diffident with his child and went away quickly. He told me that the other comrade was alright and this set my mind at rest. I was a bit staggered when I was given dark beer for my lunch. Nursing mothers got beer.

The unfortunate sallow woman, whose baby was born dead, followed me into the ward an hour or two later. She was married to a man whose wife had died, leaving him with four little children. He had married her to look after them. There was another woman with a still birth. It was her first and she had wanted the baby very badly. She cried when ours were brought in to suckle. They told her it might have been caused by inherited syphilis. She described how one evening she was sitting in her kitchen and felt a terrible coldness come over her, as though some evil had come into the kitchen. She never felt the child move again in her womb.

My baby was called Clara after Klara Zedkin, a communist member in the Reichstag. For us there were two possible girls' names: Klara or Rosa, after Rosa Luxemburg. I didn't care for Rosa as a name, so it was Clara. I wouldn't have her christened, which upset the nuns. They were very nice about it and they gave me a little book to read about St. Clara. The priest came to see me but he didn't try very hard as I think he had sized me up.

On the eighth day I went home in a taxi. It was still that lovely clear September weather. I hadn't the faintest idea what to do with a baby. We laid Clara wrapped in her beautiful white English blanket on the bed and waited for Liesle. We had paid Liesle fifty marks to come every day for a month. She wanted to buy herself a winter coat with it. She was divorced and of course unemployed. She lived in the Pankower Allee right upstairs in two rooms with her little boy Siegfried. She told me that when Siegfried was born, she had to get up a day or two after and wash the bloody sheets herself. Liesle also had Icky and his two little girls living with her. Icky used to be the porter at the house of the Rote Gewerkschaft. Before that he acted in one of the communist agitprop troupes. The troupe went to Russia on tour but when he came back he found that his wife had died. She had been pregnant and had tried to abort herself. He was left with two little girls, Karin and Helga. For a time the grandmother looked after them but she was always putting them in the orphanage as a protest if she thought she wasn't getting enough for them from the assistance board. In the end Icky took them to Liesle.

Liesle came and she showed me how to bath Clara and then cooked dinner for us: rissoles and cauliflower. I drank my dark beer. Clara thrived; she was a fat little baby and seemed to have a happy nature.

We set up a little photographic business doing portraits, mostly of children. We put up a show case downstairs outside on a wall. That was how we got to know Herr Salinger who had a chemist shop on the Grellstrasse that also sold paint. We decided on blue paint and we were rather surprised, when that evening, Herr Salinger turned up to visit us and to advise us on how best to do it. He looked like those caricatures of Germans in the First World War: plump and pink with a walrus moustache. Herr Salinger was a Jew so we got to know him well. I always bought my soap and toilet things from his shop on principle. He had an assistant, Gerda Wittenberg, a Jewish girl. She was one of those enthusiastic, rather angular people. Willi made friends with her one evening when they were both coming home on the train. She came to visit us quite a lot and we both got very fond of her. She was a socialist, communistically inclined. Her younger sister was in the Zionist movement which was still allowed in Germany 1935 and for young Jews it was the only way to have some sort of social life. Gerda wouldn't join it because she said it was a nationalist movement and that was wrong. However, in the end Willi persuaded her to join by telling her that socialists and communists should infiltrate the Zionist movement. She joined and with her sister emigrated to Palestine, thank goodness! She was saved from the gas chambers; her parents who stayed in Germany weren't. I called my second child after her.

Christmas came and Easter. On Easter morning when we opened the door, we found a whole arrangement of Easter eggs and an Easter Hare outside. It was the Cornelsons, the Nazi neighbours. She did another nice thing; she tried to get me to have Clara christened. In Germany, for a small amount of money, one could be excused from paying a Church tax; with it came a document saying you were not a Church member. However it was taken as a sign of being a communist or a socialist. When the Nazis came to power, a lot of people joined the Church again, for fear of being thought communist, and Frau Cornelson thought it would be safer for us to be in the Church; so it was a Christian action. We had a discussion about it and I, in my pig-headed way, pointed out to her that if I didn't believe in God I shouldn't be showing a lot of respect either to my own integrity or the Christian faith, if I joined to save my skin. But it was well meant. I went to tea with them once across the landing. The view from their little room down the street to the Prenzlauer Allee was practically the same as ours. We had tea or rather coffee in that room. She came once to tea with me.

In the Hedwigs hospital there was a mother whose baby was born at the same time as Clara. Frau Reitze was terribly poor and had nothing for the baby. The hospital gave her a basket and a stech kissen, a sort of double pillow in which you can tie the baby to keep it warm. I gave her some of my English things and kept up with her. Her baby, Waltraut, was a splendid child with red curls. She walked when she was ten months old and started to talk. Herr Reitze was a waiter by trade but unemployed. They lived near the Alexander Platz in two rooms on the top floor: bug ridden, water tap on the stairs half a flight below, lavatories out in the yard. Frau Reitze was sent by the N.S.V.[1] for a holiday in the Baltic, which she needed. She was sent without Waltraut who was put in a home. She took a pair of shoes which I gave her; they probably didn't fit her but she wanted smarten up and to make a good show. Waltraut, who was used to sleeping with her mother and father in their bed and being fed whenever she demanded food, became very ill and very nearly died. It is pretty staggering and fascinating that although Herr Reitze was unemployed and on the dole, the obvious solution, that he look after

1 National Socialistische Volkswolfart, government welfare organisation.

Waltraut, didn't come into the question as a possibility. Herr Reitze was a man and therefore a woman had to look after his baby for him. He only took her when she had pneumonia and he thought she was dying. Reitz visited her and found her standing up in the cot uncovered and whimpering. He took her home and nursed her back to health. Frau Reitze was on her N.S.V. holiday and couldn't come back until the end of the fortnight. Waltraut's development was retarded and she didn't start to walk or talk for about four months. Frau Reitze had another baby. She kept on coming to see me, and I invited Frau Cornelson to meet her. I thought it would do her good to meet a pure Aryan of this type who had to cope with the problems of poverty and bad housing in Hitler's Reich. It wasn't a very gay tea party. Frau Reitze had more children and in the end was re-housed in a new block of flats in Reinickendorf. Before they moved they were decontaminated. This involved them all being moved into one of their bug-ridden rooms, while the other was sealed and fumigated. Then they were moved back into that one and the other room was sealed and fumigated. This didn't really inconvenience the bugs as the one bed they slept on was not fumigated. No doubt their bugs got re-housed too.

We had the tea party in our shabby living room. We had distempered it when we moved in, but that was already three years old. We had a straw mat on the floor, it was green, no curtains; a blue linen cover on the bed. Actually I slept in that room and Willi in the other because Willi used to read very late. I was so tired when I went to bed that I liked to go to sleep at once. Later we bought lino for my room. By this time we were much more affluent and we bought inlay lino. This means that the pattern is printed right through. It is more expensive but the colours don't wear off. It was a modern design with geometrical patterns.

Willi gave up the photographic business and got a job as a building labourer. It was very heavy work and he found it too hard. From the labour exchange he was directed to a retraining course for technical draughtsmen. In Hitler's world there was no work for compositors, Willi's original profession. He enjoyed the course. They had a good lecturer who told him, among other things, that Willi's name, Jungmittag, was a very old one. It is in the Saxon Chronicle and his ancestors were Saxon robber knights. This pleased us. He then found a job with Bamag A.G. It was advertised in the Deutsche Allgemeine Zeitung. Willi never liked working in the drawing office. He used to say of his colleagues:

"Arsch lecker, arsch lecker, richtige arsch lecker."

He didn't like having his dinner in the canteen. He wanted me to bring him his dinner like his mother used to for his father. Willi's mother, Oma, cooked it and then tramped herself, or sent one of the children with it in a tin can to the workshop, where Willi's father, Opa, heated it up on the stove. I drew the line at this as it was three stations on the ringbahn and I had little children.

My husband's family came from Saxony. They had been weavers for generations back in a place called Meran not far from Leipzig. We found this out when we were getting documents to prove that we were of Aryan descent so that I could get a passport. It is rather a fascinating comment on social history that we found Willi's fore-father's birth and marriage certificates back to his great grandfather. I was quite unable to find out where my paternal grandfather was born although he was a lord. Fortunately both sets of my grandparents had been legally married in church and this was sufficient to prove Aryan descent.

Willi's father, Richard Jungmittag, was a foundry worker and Klara, his mother, was in service with an English family living in Leipzig. Willi's birth certificate says that he was born in Stotteritz by Leipzig. He was the second son and, at the time of his birth, Richard was unemployed. He was an active trade unionist and was black-listed. This meant that he could get no work in Saxony. Oma took in washing. Willi was born at seven months and he was so frail and had such a tender skin that Oma had to tear up her trousseau nightgowns to make nappies for him. Opa found a job in Bremen which, being one of the Hanseatic towns, was not so dominated by the steel barons. Oma went to the doctor to ask if she could travel with the baby. The doctor said it would probably die anyway, but the change in the air might do good. It did and he survived. In Bremen they rented a house in a little street down by the docks. It had three tiny rooms on the ground floor: a kitchen with a lavatory partitioned off, and upstairs three more tiny rooms, and a balcony over the kitchen. Two more children were born, both girls, so there were four of them: Fritz, Willi, Marriane called Mieke, and Klarchen. The babies were born at home. The midwife came for the birth but after that they had to manage. Opa put a cup of coffee by the bedside when he went to work. Oma nearly died once when her bladder, like mine, wouldn't work. In the First World War Opa was called up and she was left alone with four children. They had a little back yard and kept chickens and a pig. Oma found work in a butcher's shop. She locked the children in the house before she went to work in the morning. She would feel the hens to see if they were going to lay, so that she would know if the children had eaten the eggs. Once they managed to climb up and get sugar from the top of the cupboard but they were betrayed by Klarchen, the youngest, who stood in front of the cupboard pointing up at it and saying Ulu Ulu when Oma came home. Opa was wounded and invalided home. Towards the end of the war, when the food situation was really bad, the boys used to go out into the countryside hampstering, which was going to the farms and begging. Sometimes they got potatoes or apples or bits of old bacon. Hampstering was forbidden and the police were at the stations to catch the hampsterers. Once Willi had a whole sack of apples which a policeman took away from him, but he screamed so loudly and looked so little that the policeman gave it back to him. Willi stayed very small. After the war they had a lot of American ships in the docks bringing famine relief. One of the sailors gave Willi a watch of which he was very proud but it never worked. Both Oma and Opa were members of the Social Democratic Party and the children used to deliver Vorwarts, the S.D.P. paper. Once on his round Willi saw a woman with a nanny goat and its kid. He asked if he could have the kid. She told him to finish his round and then he could come back for it. It was a long way but when he came back she told him she had been joking and laughed.

Fritz was apprenticed to a farmer, but he didn't like it and ran away to sea. He sailed in the small tramp steamers that plied over to England and up the Norwegian coast. Willi, who was very bright, was apprenticed to a compositor. In his dinner hour he went to the central market and helped the market women. They gave him apples which he loved. He served his three year apprenticeship and then went on the Walze. That meant going on a tour around Germany, Austria and Czechoslovakia. The Trade Unions gave a mark to every Geselle[1] who came through the towns, otherwise they got work from the peasants. They slept under haystacks and in barns. Willi went right down to the mountains in Austria, visited Vienna, Prague and Berlin. It took him a year and when he came back to Bremen he got a job with Kaffee Hag in their advertising department. This was 1928 when the Bauhaus in Dessau was at the height of its fame. Kaffee Hag gave him a grant to go there and study

1 journey man

lay-out and design. It wasn't much of a grant but his parents helped him and he went. This opened up a new world for him. He made friends and joined the Communist Party. Hannes Meyer was head of the school while Kandinsky and Klee were professors. There was a very lively photographic section. Willi got keen on photography and he was brilliant at it. This made him want to be a reporter. When his year was finished he felt he couldn't bear to go back to Bremen so he came to Berlin with Ernst, who was an architectural student, and Etel, a Hungarian-Jew who had also studied photography. Ernst and Etel were married. The three of them took a flat in the same block in Tempelhof where we lived. Etel had an allowance from her family and so, I think, did Ernst. Willi started to do freelance reporting for the photographic agencies. They were in the same party branch as we were and so that is where I came in.

Willi's mother sent him parcels of food and he sent her his washing. The parcel arrived faithfully even when we were in England and often saved the situation, sausages and cake.

When we eventually did get married, which was the spring of 1933, and after we got our money sorted out, we went to Bremen to visit them. We arrived on our motor bike pop-popping in the Wiedstrasse. Klarchen was married and had a little boy called Peter. Mieke was also married and expecting her first baby. Everybody crowded in the minute front room which had a small settee, a table and a bookshelf. About five people could just squeeze themselves around the table and Oma brought in the coffee and the klaben: a sort of delicious cake. Klarchen lived upstairs and Mieke had a flat a few streets away. Fritz was engaged to be married and had bought himself a smallholding a few miles out of Bremen.

The first evening there was a row. Opa had a new wireless set and when he turned it on after supper to hear the news, it wouldn't work. He accused Auguste, Klarchen's husband, because he found a cigar stump when he opened the back. It turned out that Oma had knocked the plug out when she was laying the table for supper. Opa suspected Auguste of listening to foreign stations.

Auguste, Klarchen and Peter lived upstairs. Auguste was unemployed. He used to work on the trams but got the sack because he was a Social Democrat. Opa was alright, he worked in a small foundry which only employed three or four men. He was the foreman and friends with the boss. We didn't talk politics and when I made some comment they changed the conversation. If I persisted, Oma shut me up with, "We don't want to talk about that now."

Actually Fritz had joined the S.A. although he didn't let on to his family. After he gave up being a sailor, he found a job as a male nurse and gardener in the big Bremen mental hospital. He was sacked when Hitler came to power because his family was Social Democrat; Oma was a city councillor. He borrowed money from Opa and Oma and friends of the family and bought a smallholding just outside Bremen. Elfrieda, his fiancée, was a nurse in the hospital. She came that first evening wearing a silk dress, over which she wore a cardigan. Her hair was done in that old fashioned German style: plaits coming round on the nape of the neck under her ears. I didn't like her.

That night we slept in Oma and Opa's room; they on one end and we on the other end of their twin beds. Opa started to talk.

He just said: "It's no good going against the state, it does no good."

We didn't answer and he didn't mean us to. We just lay still in the dark. Being middle class and a communist, I had idealised the working class. I hadn't realised how desperately important it was to be respectable and to have a clean and tidy appearance, the significance of money, possessions and clothes, indeed all the paraphernalia of living; how terribly one was under observation from the rest of the street and how there were so many taboos.

Our life went on again in the Gubitzstrasse, our flat in Berlin. We had bicycles and used to ride out on Sundays to the Rieselfelde, these were sewage farms quite near the edge of town. It was flat and sometimes smelly but it was open country with hedges and trees and birds. We put Clara in a basket on the front of Willi's bike. Sometimes we went for walks in the Laubenkolonie. German allotments are a bit different to English ones. People build themselves summer houses where they live in the summer time. We made jam in the autumn which made a delicious smell in the flat. At Christmas time we had a tree and bought presents. On New Years Eve we went down to Oma and Frau Stach and celebrated the New Year, opening the window to let the New Year in, and wondering how many more years it would be until Hitler was finished.

We had a holiday every year; that was my middle class tradition. The first year after Clara was born we went to Thiessow on Rugen, an island in the Baltic, just off the coast by Stralsund. We crossed by paddle steamer. Thiessow reminded me of Ireland, although the cliffs were much lower and the sea less wild and brilliant. Our lodging was in a fisherman's house, Herr Peters. The fishermen owned the nets cooperatively and had done so since time immemorial. The place was so isolated that no feudal lord or businessman had bothered to interfere. Also Rugen had belonged to Sweden and in the Napoleonic Wars the French had occupied it. Herr Peters served in the German Navy in the First World War. It was from the Baltic fishermen that the German Navy drew its sailors. Over the mantelpiece was a photograph of the crew of the submarine in which he served and underneath was written:

"Vier lange jahr in sturm und not
jetzt haben wir unsere freiheit rot"
"Four long years in storm and danger
now we have our red freedom"

He had taken part in the revolt of the German Navy which ended the First World War. They had five children, three girls and two boys; the youngest born at the same time as Clara, a mighty baby. They had a nice house by the beach, which Herr Peters painted every year to preserve the wood from the damp climate. We had the front room and cooked in their kitchen. There was one shop in the village. Peters gave us fish, mostly sea eel with green bones but also herring. Sometimes they smoked the herrings. We collected oak twigs from a scrubby little oak grove on the cliff top. They soaked the herrings for a night in brine, and then smoked them in the open under damp sacks on a wooden frame. They tasted about as delicious as anything I have ever eaten. They had a little land and grew their own potatoes. When the boats came in with the catch, the wives had to leave whatever they were doing, it had to be the wives, and go at once to the seashore where the catch was emptied out in a heap on the beach. The women stood in a circle while the oldest walked round the circle throwing a fish in front of each wife until there were no more and each woman had a pile at her feet. All the time she sang a sort of chant. They didn't do this with the main catch which they took this over to Stralsund and sold to the dealers. They owned everything cooperatively.

It was a rather marvellous holiday. We had a wonderful thunder storm the first evening which Willi loved. It took me three hours to make up Clara's first feed but afterwards I got better at Peter's stove.

Inge the youngest girl who was five took to Willi. She stood in front of him with her clear blue eyes and said:

"Ich seuch ein brautigum"[1]

They spoke Platt Deutsch, which I could understand quite a bit as a lot of the words are very like English. The children were very free and I never heard them scolded. Once Inge fell into the sea and was only rescued by luck because some boys saw her. Like the Irish fishermen none of them could swim. There was a good deal of tension between Frau Peters and the old grandmother. We went on going there every year till 1938 and we went once more in the war in 1943. That time the photograph had disappeared from the mantelpiece and the paddle steamer wasn't running. A dyke had been built to the mainland and the train ran on into Rugen. We had to walk some miles from the station. A rainstorm came on and we sheltered with the children in the little forest by the road. And it was there in 1943 that I ate six large salted herrings in one go. They were off the ration which shows how hungry we were in the war. Our life in Berlin did seem horrid in comparison. So terribly inorganic and as far as getting rid of the Nazis, we didn't seem to be having much effect, but our belief that they couldn't last was unshakeable. It was only after Munich that I began to think about emigrating: possibly to Australia. Dreary and negative as the Nazi way of life was, the Germans seemed to like it. If the war hadn't come I think we might have emigrated. Willi felt very strongly that he was German and should stay there to take part in the revolution which would come in time. I was becoming a bit doubtful.

Klara Harprad came to see us. She wanted us to do another job for the Party. This was to photograph documents. It was exciting. The man who we were to do it for came to see us. Willi went with him and bought some strong lamps but in the end nothing happened.

I was twice pregnant and twice had an abortion. I wanted another child but we thought it irresponsible to have children as we should always be ready to work for the Party however dangerous it might be. Having abortions was partly bravado with me and partly an expression of my rejection and contempt for Nazi Germany. It was still possible though much more dangerous than in the old days. Mine was done by a lady doctor who was unable to practice because she was Jewish. She had fallen back on this to make a living. She had to do it without anaesthetic because she was afraid that one would shout out. She did my

1 I'm looking for a bridegroom

abortion which was exceedingly painful and very unpleasant, particularly the second time. Because I wanted to have another child I had to steel myself to have it done. I went alone to the doctor to where she lived in Wilmersdorf, the other side of Berlin. I rested after it for about an hour before I went home by the Ringbahn. I was afraid to take a taxi in case it was noticed. Not long after she was betrayed by one of her patients. She was arrested and hanged herself in her prison cell.

In the end I did have another child. I didn't think an only child was a good thing. We felt that even if the war came, and we still hoped it wouldn't, with two children the family would be a better unit and more able to stand up to stresses. It took quite a long time before anything happened, about a year. I had the mumps and I don't know whether this affected my fertility. My second child was conceived in February 1939 and born in November. All my pregnancies, except the first, would have been born in the autumn. I was very well, much healthier than when Clara was on the way. We were much better off as Willi was earning about 180 marks a month and I was still getting my English money which was about the same. Our rent was 72 marks a month, this included heating and hot water. Gas and electricity between them cost about another 12 to 15 marks a month. The cost of living was stable and we could buy things. We bought a tent and Willi bought himself a Klepper mantel made from one of the first plastic materials. They were raincoats and they looked very good and smart. We went for our summer holiday to the Baltic but not to Thiessow this time as we thought we'd have a change. We went to Prerow on the mainland. The idea was to camp with our tent and to hire a boat if possible. The first night in the tent there was a frightful thunderstorm and it rained buckets. The tent held out alright, but camping with a small child isn't a pleasure and I was five months pregnant so we gave up and took a room in the village. Willi went fishing up the river and Clara and I sat on the sands. The morning after that wet night we made friends with a barge family who were always moving around. They had a little boy about eight years old who had to learn to fight because, always being a stranger, the other boys set on him. His mother was rather a splendid Brechtian character. She told us how when he first came crying to her she gave him no sympathy.

"Du hast auch Hände" she said.[1]

1 Thou also hast hands

She gave Clara raw potatoes which she liked. We rolled up our splendid tent to an audience of children.

I went to England for a final visit. It was the beginning of August and I took Clara with me. I half hoped the war would break out while I was there. Everybody was very kind. A rich aunt gave me the most lovely quilted red silk dressing gown. I gorged myself on fruit and butter and bought back a supply of Crooks Halibut Oil Capsules. I went back from Harwich. Nan Robertson and her husband drove me to the docks. We had spent a lovely few days with them in their comfortable house in the magic Suffolk countryside. Nan was a beautiful driver. She drove us through the Suffolk splashes; Clara loved it. I walked onto the ship and was alone with Europe.

Back in Berlin, Oma and Opa came to stay. We took them to Potsdam which they liked very much. It was obvious that the war was coming. Opa sat smoking his cigar in our living room after breakfast.

"Die Deutscher sind eine Kriegerische Rasse"[1] he said proudly and rather provocatively to me. He was such a comic little specimen, he looked like Popeye, that I held my peace. There wasn't much point in having a row. We took them to the station to get the train back to Bremen. It was very full and they pushed their way on, desperately clutching their suitcases. They wouldn't leave go of them although we told them to get seats and we'd hand them up to them. We watched the train move out with Oma waving her handkerchief.

1 The Germans are a warlike race

Chapter 3 Berlin 1939-1944

Rationing started before the war but semi-rationing by the shops had been going on for quite a long time. You could only buy butter and fats in shops that knew you: about half a pound a week. The first real rations were very small indeed: an eighth of a pound of butter per week and no other fats. The authorities reckoned that everybody would have laid in stocks, which of course they had. One bought anything one could lay one's hands on, soap, fats, sugar, coffee, tinned things. I bought an enormous tin of furniture polish and a long brush to scrub one's back with; something I would never have gone in for in normal times. For us there was another problem: money. My income was finished so we were down to Willi's salary.

The war came and in a way we were glad. On that particular Sunday, which was fine Berlin September weather, we went with Clara in the push chair to the Rehburg Park. We sat on the grass. They had a big white board like a cricket scoring board and the news was written up on it. We saw England had declared war. That was it.

I was afraid that all the hospitals would be requisitioned for the army, so I went to the midwife on the Grellstrasse to find out about it. I found a bed in the Kaiserin Augusta Victoria Krankenhause. It was over in the west end near the Tiergarten. When I went there for checkups it always reminded me of Axel; it was his part of Berlin.

After the first weeks the rations got better. We had paper ration cards given out every four weeks by the Nazi party block wardens. They were about 6 by 4 inches and different colours; blue for meat, yellow for fats, pink for bread, white for sugar and mauve for cereals, coffee and extra things like jam. Coffee was of course ersatz coffee. We had no real coffee or tea at all except for a special Christmas bonus. Of course there was a black market. Later on in the war the prices were fantastic: the equivalent of about thirty English pounds for half a pound of butter or a quarter of coffee. Nevertheless the rations were honoured right through until the end of the war. The card distributors must have done fairly well. Klara Harprad had a brother in Westphalia who was a teacher. The ration cards were laid out in the schools ready for the Nazi block wardens. He managed to take about half a dozen cards from each pile every

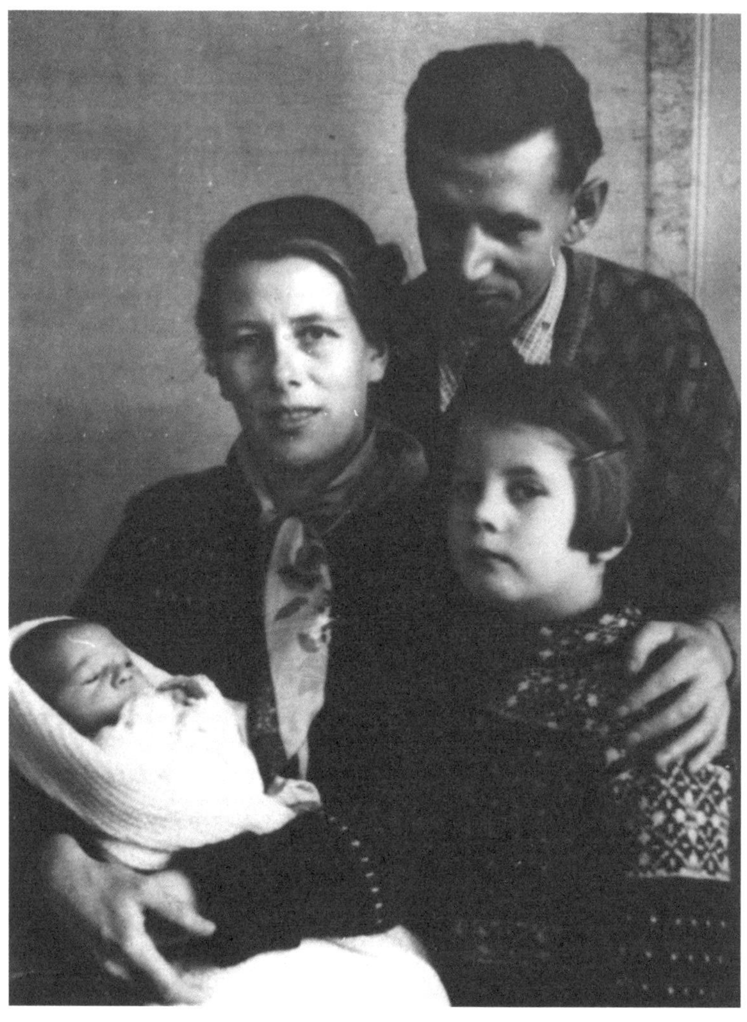

Biddy, Willi, Gerda, the baby, and Clara aged 5 years. Berlin, Christmas 1939

month right through the war. It was never noticed so they must have allowed extras for the distributors. There is a German saying;

'Wer an der Quelle sitzt durstet nicht'[1]

He sent them to Klara by post which was a bit of a risk. She used them for comrades who were living illegally. It is a comment on the difference between English and German mentality that Klara would also use them for herself. She would have given me some but I wouldn't use them for us; partly because I thought it was wrong and partly because I was afraid. I didn't want to go to a concentration camp for that. On the other hand when Klara's baby was born and she stayed with me, there were various forms to fill in which had to be signed. I went to the Food Office to do this for her. It was just routine and I said to Klara that I would forge her signature for her. She was horrified and wouldn't let me do it.

At first money worried me most. Also I thought that Willi was sure to be called up and managing alone would be grim. I had friends in the house, Frau Zuhlke who lived under us, and Frau Richter who lived where Arno used to be. On our floor at the top we had a new neighbour: Herr Peters. The Cornelsons had gone back to Hamburg. They went at the time of the Munich Crisis. All their furniture went about 4 o'clock in the afternoon and they had to wait in the empty rooms until 10 o'clock at night for the train to Hamburg. Nobody, none of their party friends asked them in for a cup of coffee. I would have done but we had friends and we were all listening to the BBC, so I couldn't. They just sat there in the empty flat until it was time to go. I never heard what happened to them in the war. Frau Richter was glamorous looking, dark and tall. Her husband had a car, still a pretty unheard of thing in the Gubitzstrasse. He worked in one of the big mens clothing chain stores. He was called up right away and she was left on her own. She made friends with Frau Zuhlke. We all three of us were anti Nazi and listened to the BBC. Herr Zuhlke was afraid and tried to discourage his wife. He didn't trust Frau Richter.

On the 20th November there was the attempt on Hitler's life in the Munich beer cellar. I went down every day to get the milk as it wasn't delivered in this part of Berlin. That morning I saw that all the papers were sold out so I thought the war in the west had started in earnest.

1 Who sits at the well doesn't thirst

I went into the milk shop and said something like, "Now it's started." I felt terrible that my own people were being killed. This remark had serious consequences for me later.

Three days later I started labour. Frau Zuhlke took Clara for me and Frau Richter came with me to the hospital. We took a taxi as Willi had gone to work. I got there about eleven o'clock in the morning. The pains hadn't really come on but we had been told to go at once in, case of air raids. They made me walk about the corridors. I telephoned Willi to let him know. About 6 o'clock in the evening they gave me quinine injections and the labour really started. I had taken a detective story to read; a sort of bravado because I couldn't really read it. This time I was the only person in the ward. I made them give me an anaesthetic. I didn't see why one should go through all that agony. At midnight Gerda was born. I could see the clock. The midwife washed me. She was very good and had the most wonderful firm touch. I thought I would be able to rest as I had after Clara's birth, but I hadn't reckoned with the after pains which were much worse after the second child.

After Gerda was born they put me in a ward with eleven women. Most of the time the radio was on with the news bulletins. The song, 'Wir fahren gegen Engeland'[1] was played after each report of British ships sunk; definitely depressing. The nursing was much rougher than it had been in Hedwigs hospital, but there was one very nice big nurse with a huge bosom. She was young and made jokes about it. Klara Harprad and Frau Zuhlke came to see me. Oma came from Bremen to look after Clara and Willi. When she came to visit Oma always went through everything. I think this was normal German practice but I did resent it a bit. She found some pepper in my kitchen cupboard. The point was that in the war there was no pepper. I had this hoard because I always used to buy pepper when people came to the door selling things. It was a way of begging which people did in England too during the Depression. Pepper was the easiest thing to buy for ten pfennigs. I poured it into a tin and, as we used very little, over the years the tin became full so I had a treasure. The woman lying in the bed next to me had mentioned that she had no pepper and I had promised her some before I realised that Oma wanted it. Oma was furious; to give such riches away, out of the family to a stranger, was unforgivable. I had promised

1 We are going into England

and I wouldn't break my promise so in the end I divided my pepper into three parts. I came home in a taxi, Oma, Willi, the baby Gerda and me. Clara who had stayed with Frau Zuhlke was there to welcome us. As we got out of the taxi she wanted to carry the baby. I should have let her but she was only five. I believe there is an ancient Sicilian custom that when a new baby is born, the father puts it into the arms of the eldest child; sounds good psychology to me. Poor Clara had a nasty fall while I was in hospital. She helped Frau Zuhlke clear out her cellar and came a nasty cropper but she was alright. Oma went back to Bremen the next day. She was too worried to leave Opa and the house in case of air raids.

I was really weak and found myself crying for no reason. I didn't have enough milk and Gerda couldn't digest the usual baby diet of milk and strained oat meal. My old doctor came to see us and suggested a feed of butter and wheat flour browned in the frying pan and then diluted with milk and water; half and half. This worked and her dysentery cleared up. It was very cold as the flats had no coal so the central heating wasn't working. Hoar frost formed on the walls. We only had the old electric fire that we bought in Düsseldorf and the gas oven in the kitchen.

Our rations were not good; nothing extra for nursing mothers except milk. Later in the war they gave pregnant women and nursing mothers extra fats, bread and cereals as well as milk. I struggled hard to get my milk back and succeeded partially. I was worried about rickets because there was no orange juice nor cod liver oil. You could get Vigantol, which was a synthetic vitamin D, and Gerda had lots of it. About three weeks after Gerda was born I received a letter from the Gestapo telling me to come for an interview at the Alexanderplatz Central Police Station. I didn't know what it was about and I hoped it might be something fairly routine about letters I had been getting from my family. I took all the letters with me to show they were purely personal. The interview was in the morning at eight o'clock. I phoned the telephone number on the letter and said I had a new born baby and couldn't leave it for too long. The officer told me to get a neighbour in to look after the baby. He said he would take me first and try to let me get home as soon as possible. This sounded reassuring, but of course we were very frightened. I arranged with Frau Zuhlke to come up and give Gerda her ten o'clock feed and see after Clara. I was to drop my key into her letter box when I went. However, the evening before every thing sounded very quiet in their flat which was under ours. I went down and knocked at the door.

Herr Zuhlke was there and he told me his wife had gone to visit her mother without telling me; she had been afraid. Clara had German measles and Frau Zuhlke had a baby so I suppose it was a combination of the two things. I never forgave her. I went across to the Langemarkstrasse and found Frau Herzog. She had a little girl to whom I taught English. She also did our big washing for us in the electric laundry in her block of flats. She had been a nurse and then married. Her daughter Liselotte was a handsome child with thick black plaits. Frau Herzog came and looked after the children. I gave her my key. Why didn't Willi stay with the children? In Germany a man had to go to work unless he was ill and my husband accepted this discipline; women just had to manage. My husband didn't stay at home when I started labour or for any reason regarding me or the children. Also in this case we were afraid that at work they might find out about the visit to the Gestapo and that had to be avoided at all costs. I took the tram to Alexanderplatz. In the Polezei Presidium there was a long queue of people waiting in the corridor. On the window ledge were lots of rolls of toilet paper, a completely unobtainable commodity for ordinary citizens. I didn't pinch any because I was too frightened, also because I hadn't learned 'organisation'. Later in the war I became better at it. I had an illustrated paper with me; again this was a sort of bravado to give me confidence. I couldn't really concentrate to read it. Actually I didn't have to wait for more than a few minutes. The Gestapo man was as good as his word and really did see me first. He didn't seem to be a bad sort of chap, middle-aged and quiet. I had the impression that he was one of the older policemen who had served before Hitler. It was a fairly ordinary sort of office. It had two desks; my man sat at one of them and there was a chair for the person being interviewed by the desk. He told me to sit down and started taking particulars. I had bought all my letters which he brushed these aside and said I was perfectly entitled to correspond about personal matters with my family in England so it wasn't that. Then he asked me my maiden name. I told him that it was Macnaghten and said it was a funny name and spelled it for him, adding that it was Irish. Then he asked me where I was on the 20th November. I replied that I was at home as it was just before the baby was born. He got up and went out of the room. I could just manage to read on his desk the papers, which he had left open, and make out that my milk shop woman had denounced me for the attempt on Hitler in the Munich cellar. He came back and said I could go home. He asked me about my father and if he lived in Ireland. I lied and said, "Yes he had a home there." The point was that a thousand-mark reward had been offered for any information that would lead to the discovery of the plotters and my milk woman, knowing that I was English and not a Nazi, thought she might be lucky. Hundreds of people must have been denounced in this way. Had I not had the baby and an Irish name I don't know if I would have been alright. I did have to go six weeks later again and saw a much nastier official who told me that my answers had not been satisfactory, and if I was caught again saying anything, I would be sent to a concentration camp. When I was questioned I wouldn't make any servile remarks about the 'Fuhrer'. They would have stuck in my throat. I changed my milk woman and that was that. I went to Frau Zuhlke's milk shop further down the Grellstrasse, owned by a jolly soul who had buried three husbands and took another one at the age of sixty. She had the strange shape that Berliner milk shop women always seemed to develop; very wide and bulgy, their white overalls bring it out.

Christmas came and the flats got some coal and it wasn't so cold. At New Year, as usual, we opened the window to let the New Year in and wondered how much longer. We decided we must have a holiday. We still had about 150 marks saved up. I weaned Gerda. She was six months old. I felt that feeding her was sapping all the strength out of me. We went for our holiday in May to a little village on the Oder River. We went by train and then by bus. We had the address from a colleague of Willi's in the drawing office.

The house where we stayed belonged to a widow and her daughter. They did the cooking so I did really have a rest. I lay in the garden on a deck chair and read German love stories. In Germany in those days they didn't have detective stories; I don't know if they have them yet. Willi went fishing and caught an enormous pike. We had a photograph of him and Clara and the pike which was longer than Clara.

It was the time of the invasion of France and Dunkirk. The people where we stayed were Nazis. They were cock-a-hoop. We couldn't say what we thought. Having lived in France and knowing the country, I was miserable. I had studied in Paris for three years and spent one summer in Avignon. But of course we still enjoyed the sun. We went with the children to the Oder to bathe. Gerda was very fair and her sunburnt head showed through her wispy bleached hair; she was getting on very well.

We did have one argument with our hostesses about the Japanese. They said they were a more pure race than the Chinese; well I suppose they had to be, being allies.

We came back to Berlin. Klara Harprad was pregnant; she always wanted to have a baby. She had an old friend Arnold, who was a soldier. He came back on leave to Berlin, stayed with her, and her son Veit was the result. However, in the autumn before he was born, her school was evacuated to Poland. They went to a place in West Poland near Posnan. It was a great house that had belonged to some Polish aristocrat. The children were quartered in the stables. They arrived there in October and it was already beginning to get cold. The first night they had no blankets. They got them the next night but no sheets for six weeks. Klara described how the cook, who was Polish, had to stand by the stove working although she had had peritonitis and she still had a tube in her stomach draining the wound. Her husband had been taken to Sachsenhausen concentration camp where he died. One of the girls had a skin disease. Her hair had to be washed every night and her head oiled with olive oil. The teachers, who had rooms in the great house, had to do this. Klara came back just before Christmas because her baby was due in March. We had a great feast with a fillet of roast pork. She taught me how to make a pudding. You boiled up a packet of flavoured cornflour with milk and water and just as it went off the boil you added the yolk of an egg and then the white whipped up stiff. We used to have about one egg a week; it was a great delicacy.

That Christmas we went to Bremen and stayed with Fritz on his farm. Elfrieda was expecting her second baby. While we were there one of the pigs swallowed something that stuck in its throat. Late at night they had to get the butcher to slaughter it. We stood in the byre by the light of an oil lamp to watch it. It was like a Rembrandt picture. The byre and the house were all under the same roof. The village Meinerhausen was built in the Dutch style with houses all along the road and behind them long strips of land back to where there was still uncut peat. Fritz had two mental patients from the hospital where they used to work. He was paid 60 marks each for them. The woman, who had gone mad after her seventh child, did the work in the house. I thought the man was pretty frightening and Fritz said that once he tried to attack him with a pitchfork. The two of them had their meals together in the kitchen, and we in the living room. They sat each side of the table, each alone, it looked terrible. We came back to Berlin.

Veit was born the end of March and Klara came to stay with us so I could look after him when she was at school. Veit was rather a miserable little baby. Klara was thirty-nine when he was born. He couldn't lift his head at first. She was a fussy mother but she had lots of milk and Veit was entirely breast fed. She was terribly worried when he had no motions and wanted to give him something to bring it about. I restrained her, telling her categorically that with breast fed babies it didn't matter. On the third day we found a beautiful golden stool in his nappy and she calmed down. Veit thrived. Klara was very finicky about everything. She rinsed the nappies one by one and ironed them. When she went back to school I had to give him his morning feed. He had two courses: sieved vegetables and then rhubarb for pudding with a drink of fruit juice. He had to be exposed to the sun every day for exactly so many minutes. Once I forgot and left him for about an hour. When I remembered, I rushed into the room afraid he would be burnt to a frazzle, but all was well. I never told Klara. We got on pretty well but she thought I was awfully messy; which was true. At the end of July she went home to her flat and we went on holiday. I had developed hay fever and eczema on my legs.

The war in the east had begun. We lived just by the ringbahn and had seen the troop trains going east every day. Rumour had it that the Russians were going to lay a narrow gauge on their railway[1] and let the Germans through to attack the Middle East and cut off the oil supplies to England. Willi Schuerman came to visit us a day or two before Russia was invaded and explained that Germany would attack Russia. He said this because of some report from Turkey and he was right. I was too tied up looking after the children to follow what was happening. We did listen to the BBC every evening. We tried listening to Moscow but it was much more difficult to get. Once we did get it but they were broadcasting a fashion show which put us off. The night the Germans attacked Russia, Willi had cycled out to the village on the Oder where we went on our holiday the year before. He wanted to fix it up again, but they wouldn't take us. The next morning we heard the news over the radio that the invasion had begun. I met Frau Schroede in the Hof.[2] It had

1 Russian rails have a wider gauge that European ones

2 the garden in the centre of the apartment block

been turned into allotments and we both had one. She was crying.

"Now" she said "the war will never end."

I think many Germans felt like this about it. A two-fronted war again. However the first news was very good for Germany. German troops advancing: all Russian resistance broken down, the tonnage figures of all the ships sunk in the Atlantic, and so on and so on. Yet we never for one moment believed that Germany could win the war. We never considered the idea, although at one time I thought England might be occupied. I realised that it would be impossible for the Germans to feed England, even if they wanted to. All the other countries had been self-sufficient in food production and in all these countries there were terrible food shortages because the Germans took their food. Apart from the government taking supplies, every soldier looted something.

We went for our holiday. Friedel Kopitch, who had been one of our witnesses when we were married, had a cousin who owned a farm near Frankfurt on the Oder. We had been there once for a weekend. I gave Friedel a shoe docket and she arranged for us to go. We took the train to Frankfurt. It was very crowded. From Frankfurt we had to walk as the shortage of petrol had cut buses. It was about nine miles and we had the push chair. On one side of the road was the forest and on the other side the pale August fields. We arrived at the farm about 4 o'clock. It was an old water mill with the forest was all around it.

Friedel's cousin used to have a farm in the Polish Corridor. They moved when it became part of Poland after the First World War. She was a widow. Her two elder sons were away in the army and only the youngest was at home. They had two Polish slave workers. After we'd had coffee I took Clara into the farmyard barn to show her the cows. It was rather dark and I could see not clearly. Vladec, one of the Poles was standing there. There was something wrong with one of his eyes. He told me afterwards it had happened on the transport. They were packed so tightly into the railway wagons that some of them died. He received a blow on the eye, but apart from that and getting frostbite on one foot from going barefoot in the German winter, he was all right. He came from the land and understood farm work and he was a strong, very fine looking boy. I think he was seventeen. Friedel's cousins weren't bad to their Poles and of course they spoke Polish, having come from the Corridor. They ate with the family in the kitchen, which was against the law. They slept in the cellar of the house and they had a stove; this too was against the law. Polish slave workers were not to be allowed in the house. They were supposed to live, eat and sleep in the byre with the animals. Also she tried to get boots for them but this was very difficult. All clothing was rationed and there was no allowance for Polish slave workers. She gave them her cigarette ration and she gave them food. Vladec was fairly all right but the other one wasn't. I can't remember his name. He was small and he came from Lodz where he was a factory worker. He wasn't strong and he didn't understand farm work. He was in the middle of a nervous breakdown. He couldn't look after himself; he just wandered around smoking whenever he could get anything to smoke. His clothing was utterly filthy and ragged. He had a tattered pocket book and in it a photo of a girl. He kept showing it to us saying, "That's my girl, my girl in Poland."

At the time I thought it was just the photograph of a film star, but I expect it was his girl. The point was that even I had become conditioned in my ideas so that I didn't believe a Polish girl could look smart and be nicely dressed. I'd been in Poland and knew that Poles generally are very smart and good at their appearance. We gave him as many cigarettes as we could. Having hay fever it wasn't much of a sacrifice for me as I couldn't smoke anyway and Willi didn't smoke much either. Cigarettes were of course rationed: twelve a day for a man and six for a woman until she was fifty. After that she didn't get any unless she had a son at the front. Then she was allowed them; the idea being that she sent them to him.

We weren't the only summer guests. There were two typists from Berlin; very smart in their sun suits and perms and sunglasses. They saw the Poles in rags and believed what the Goebels propaganda told them, that the Poles were sub-human. I tried to explain it to them, but it was a waste of time. One of the sons came on leave, a stocky young man, rather solid. The girls went hay making with him; one could hear their screams (of joy) as he jumped them off the hay wagon. I sat mostly in the garden with Gerda while Clara went fishing with Willi. There was a little lake up on the heath, silent and wind blown. We went into the forest and picked blueberries and mushrooms.

One evening the farmer's wife made us blueberry soup and Clara spilt the whole of hers over the table cloth. This was terrible because it stains. When we were back in Berlin I sacrificed clothing coupons and bought her a new one. They had a cousin staying there, a retired policeman. He was very outspoken. He said the French prisoners get their Red Cross parcels and clothing so the Poles ought to have theirs. If they work they should have the clothing they need.

I told Vladec I was English, and he confided in me that he was going to run away and join the resistance. I thought of the grizzly tales we had heard of how the Germans, when they caught the Polish Resistance fighters, hung them up with their feet just touching the ground so it took ages for them to die.

I said "Don't, the war can't last for ever; here at least you have food. Wait."

He said "I have boots in Poland. My mother has my boots."

He did run away later. I met Friedel a few months later and she told me.

"So ungrateful," she said "after what we did for him."

Our holiday was over. The last night Willi and Vladec caught some frogs and put them in the girls' beds, which made them scream some more. They blamed it on Vladec, and were rather surprised when Willi owned up to this good old German practical joke. The old policeman drove us in the farm wagon with two horses through the forest to the station. Vladec came a little way with us, running behind. We saw him the last time, standing in the shadow of the trees, by the side of the track.

Back to Berlin, raids, dust, noise. My hay fever was still not better, so I went to the doctor. He cauterised my nose with a wire; at least, I think that is what he did. Anyway he stuck a wire up it and gave me infra-red treatment and a special orange ointment which he said was supposed to be only used for soldiers. It healed my nose and I got better.

We received some furniture. Grete had a Jewish friend. She was an old woman called Frau Grunewald who had been turned out of her flat. Jews were turned out of Neu Bau as these were modern flats with central heating. She had nowhere to store her furniture, so we took some of it: two splendid cupboards. We had one in the kitchen and one in Willi's room. She was rather frail and came to see us. She wore the star, of course, but she wasn't one to cover it up with holding her handbag over it. The star was about four inches across, made of yellow material and had to be on all clothes worn out of doors. I made a rice pudding with milk for her. Jews got no milk, not even skimmed and not even for children. They also had no clothing coupons and no shoe dockets so everything had to be obtained through friends or on the black market which was very expensive. We discussed the war and said that if we all survived she would take the furniture back. We arranged that I was to send any children's shoes I could lay my hands on to a farm where she was living. It was owned previously by the Jewish community. They had an agricultural school to teach people who were emigrating to Palestine. The Nazis had taken it over but some Jews were allowed to work there. She had collected as many Jewish children as she could and taken them out to the farm; I think she had seven or eight. About a year later she and all the children were brought back to Berlin. They spent one night in the collection station, sleeping on the floor, and then were sent off on the transport. We didn't know where they had been sent and we didn't know about the gas chambers. I just thought they died of exhaustion, exposure and starvation. She wanted to take Clara for a walk, but I thought this was a mistake, because of the neighbours and the star, and didn't let her. She gave me a map of London and a copy in English of George Burrows 'Lavengro', which she treasured. She had friends in England and had stayed with them in Welwyn Garden City.

Clara was seven and started school. In Germany children started school between the ages of five-and-a-half and six-and-a-half. Clara's birthday was in September and normally she would have gone to school at Easter. That year the children started in the autumn instead of Easter. This was done because many of the schools were used by the army and the ones still in use were terribly overcrowded. Our school was used by the army so she had to go to one in the Greifswalderstrasse. The school had three shifts: eight to eleven, eleven to two and two to five o'clock. Clara's teacher had three classes of fifty school beginners. My friend Klara, who was a teacher, had rubbed into me that I mustn't teach Clara to read before she went to school or she would be bored in class. I didn't, and Clara was not one of those children who learn to read by themselves. At first I didn't help her but Fraulein Jung, the teacher, asked me to come and see her. She told me that Clara was not doing as well as she should. Did I help her? I said no. She pointed out that it was absolutely impossible to for her to teach one hundred and fifty children with two and a half hours to do it in, and if I didn't teach Clara, nobody would. I saw her point. Fraulein Jung used to write up a dictation on the board for the children to copy on their slates. They had gone back to slates to save paper. Clara brought this home and practised writing it. The next day Fraulein Jung dictated it to the class and they had to write it. She

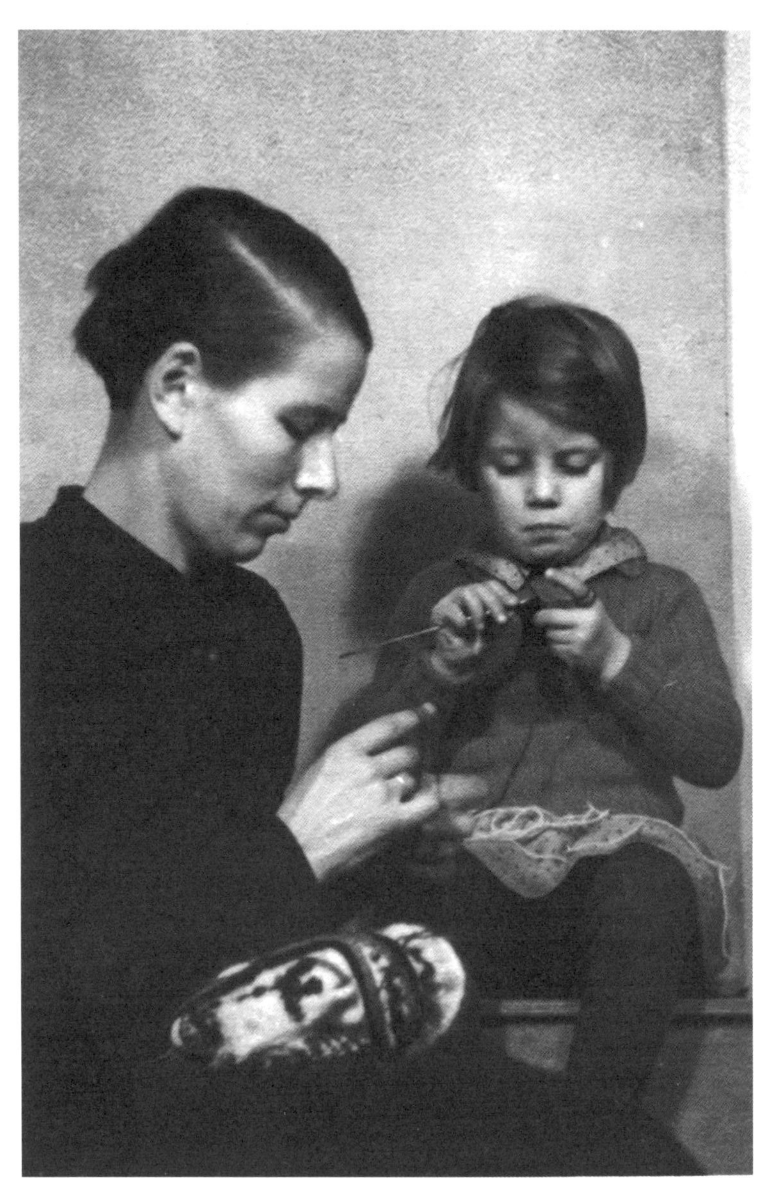

Biddy with Clara learning to knit, Berlin 1940

was a conscientious teacher and did her best under impossible conditions. Clara learned to read and write in a year. The first year they still used Gothic letters, which I wasn't very good at. The following year Germany changed to Latin script, which is the same as ours. I suppose they thought that if they were going to conquer the world, Germans had better write in a script that subject nations could read. Clara had trouble with arithmetic, so we made her a card with dots in groups of ten which we could partly cover. This taught her to add and subtract. Later in England Clara did very well at school, passing her A-levels in four subjects, in spite of not learning English until she was eleven. I think this shows that it doesn't matter starting formal education late, in fact, it may be a good thing.

In August, after we came back from our holiday and just before she started school, Clara was ill. One Saturday night she came out with a lump on her neck and she had a temperature. I couldn't get our doctor because it was Saturday, so the relief one came. He said he thought it was scarlet fever. I was to watch her carefully and see if she peeled. He said that sometimes children with scarlet fever had a rash that one hardly noticed, and afterwards had a sort of glandular fever. I was very worried because I was afraid that if I caught it I would have to go to hospital and there would be nobody to look after the children. In the street two children had died of it. I watched Clara, but she didn't peel. She went on having the lump on her neck and a fever for six weeks. We had a lot of raids at that time and had to carry Clara down to the cellar nearly every night. We didn't go to the main cellar with the others. The Nazis in this cellar were horrid to Clara and wouldn't let her join in any of the games with the other children to pass away the time during the long air raids. Our cellar was in what had been the laundry and drying room of the flats; it was semi-basement. At the beginning of the war the windows were blocked up and they put in gas filters. These were never fitted properly and we just had a sort of drain pipe attached to the blocked up windows. Frau Zinz, who was Jewish with an Aryan husband, had to go with her half-Jewish children into a little cellar next to ours. Clara just got better and her lump disappeared. One morning her temperature went down and she was herself again. One moment I got so worried that I asked our doctor, (she was a woman, and good) if Clara oughtn't to go into hospital. She turned on me, her eyes literally blazing, and said do you want her in hospital where she'll pick up every disease going. She was quite right; in those days it was best to keep out of hospital. I bought Clara a pair of new stockings. She was so pleased with them; it seemed to contribute to her cure. For her birthday I bought her a plastic cape; it was a bright greeny-blue turquoise colour. We could afford to buy so few things that it was a great event, and I was very proud of it.

Fritz and Elfrieda came to stay; they were on their way to Poland. Fritz had a job in Poland. Elfrieda had dabbled in the black market and Fritz was scared. It was very dangerous and you could get a death sentence. Elfrieda's sister was a Nazi youth leader and Fritz got the job through her. When the Russians made their pact with the Germans certain parts of Bessarabia in Romania went to the Soviet Union and certain parts remained in German-controlled areas. The peasants who didn't want to be in the Soviet Union could opt out. The Germans settled them on Polish farms. The Romanian farmers didn't understand how to farm Polish land; it was more northerly, and Fritz had the job of agricultural adviser. He first went alone and used to stay the night with us on the way. The first time he came he bought us about eighty eggs. He wanted a camera for them, but we only had an old Leica and an old Rolleiflex. Willi wouldn't give them up so we rather meanly took the eggs and gave Fritz nothing for them. After about a year, Elfrieda decided to join him with the children and let their small holding at Meinershausen. They spent the night with us. They went out for the evening and I put the children, Richard and Helga, to bed. When I undressed them, and was going to take off their vests, Richard told me that they didn't ever take them off. I was surprised although I now know that it isn't only Germans who do this. In my bigoted fashion, I put it down to another dirty habit of the German master race. Elfrieda, when she was going in the morning, said to me, "In Poland it's a wonderful life, Brigitte, not a stroke of work from morning to night." I thought, you wait my girl, your life of luxury with Polish slave workers won't last long; and it didn't. Fritz had a very nasty cough and it turned out to be tuberculosis. By the time he went to the doctor he was pretty far gone. He was sent to the hospital in Poland and had an operation; I suppose to collapse his lung but, whether on purpose or by mistake, the operation went wrong. It was said that they cut the stomach nerve instead of the lung nerve. This sounds odd to me; anyway he was thought to be dead and put into the mortuary. He wasn't dead and lived for about another six months. He told us about the evacuation of the Polish farmers. There was a curfew every night. About an hour after the curfew the S.S. would go to the farm, getting wagons from the neighbouring ones, and then it would be:

"Raus, raus ihr schwein",[1] and the people would be out in half an hour, whether the woman was in childbirth, or anybody was sick. They were only allowed to take personal clothing and cooking pots. They were driven to the collecting station and then divided into 'German friendly' and 'German unfriendly' peasants. The latter were sent to concentration camps and almost certainly died. The 'German friendly' were sent to Germany: the men to Saxony to work as farm labourers and the women and children to Bremen and Berlin to work in factories. They lived in barracks, often where bombing was severe. Fritz thought this was awful. He said the families that were separated had no means of knowing what had happened to each other; the fathers: the fate of their families, and the wives: the fate of their man. He made a lot of money on the side by warning the Polish farmers when their turn was coming. He paid off his mortgage on Meinershausen in about a year. He also told us how he had killed a man. It was his job to go round the farms and check that the peasants were delivering all their grain. Once he went to a farm and climbed into the loft to see. The farmer went in front of him; Fritz saw him stoop down to pick something up. He shot the man out of hand. He said the man had a revolver there on the floor, and had meant to kill him; nevertheless, I think it shocked him.

After Fritz died, Elfrieda didn't get much pension which disgusted her. She saw the red light in the end and went back to Bremen. She had Fritz's body brought back to Bremen and re-interred. They had a ceremony and the coffin was lowered into the grave with a swastika flag over it. My sisters-in-law wouldn't attend, but Oma and Oma went; Fritz was Oma's favourite. Klarchen, my sister-in-law, let her son Peter attend the Fuhrerschule. This was a special school for Aryan youth who were to learn how to be elite leaders. Peter was blonde with blue eyes.

The next summer 1943 we went again to Thiessow for our holiday. We financed our holiday by borrowing from our neighbours on the Grellstrasse. They were extraordinarily kind. Herr Zimmerman had a small linen factory in Pomerania, and they had a little boy the same age as Clara. They used to give us fish too which Herr Zimmerman brought back from Pomerania. His factory was on the coast. We paid them back

1 Get out you pigs

over the year and then borrowed again for the next holiday. They hated fascism and anti-Semitism and I suppose it was partly because I was English that they were so kind. The thing I remember most about that holiday was getting off-the-ration salt herrings and eating five straight off. I was hungry. The rations weren't enough and hunger built up and up. Fritz twice sent us a turkey from Poland for Christmas. We invited all our friends and had a feast. We felt full for about two hours and then it wore off and we were hungry again. Once Grete obtained some coffee on the black-market. It was unroasted so we roasted it in the frying pan. I was half-paralysed for about two hours. My body was quite unable to cope with it. We had neither tea nor coffee all through the war, only ersatz coffee.

After we got back from Thiessow, Emil and Mieke from Bremen came to stay for a week. This was July 1943 when the raids on Bremen were much worse than on Berlin and people had lost their nerve. They told us how the asphalt streets burned. While they were still with us we received the news that all Berlin schools were to be evacuated. We had been out to the Grunewald; I remember walking home under the lime trees along the road to the station. We went to a restaurant for a drink and when we came out Mieke opened her bag and gave me two teaspoons she had taken from the table. "There you are Brigitte," she said, "There's some spoons for you." One couldn't buy cutlery or cups, and our stocks were very low. I was a bit surprised as she was so eminently respectable, but I took them. This was called 'organising'. It had been a very pleasant day but when we returned home we found the leaflet under the door which said that the schools were to be evacuated. Mothers and young children could go with the school. We sat in the little room that overlooked the Hof. It smelt rather deliciously of onions which we had harvested and hung up to dry on a string. Mieke thought I oughtn't to go and that the wife should stay with the husband. They had sent Werner, their little boy, to Saxony. I didn't like the idea of sending the children alone, and I really had had about enough of Berlin, of having to pack things ready every night, and dragging the children down to the cellar. Emil and Mieke went back to Bremen the next day.

There was a meeting in the school for the parents about the evacuation. We were given a sort of pep talk by a Nazi official. He said "It's a scandal. The German Army stands from Norway to the Pyrenees, yet there's not one Frenchman who doesn't believe that Germany will lose the war, and many of our own people in their hearts believe the same." I thought, you've said it chum. We decided it was better to go. Willi would have a better chance alone if the raids became worse.

The transport went from the Frankfurter Allee Ringbahn station. We had to be there by 9 a.m. We got everything packed. Willi made me take as much as possible, including my ski trousers. We set the alarm and then over slept, but we still had time. Willi came with us to the Frankfurter Allee. He and Clara took the two heavy cases up to the Prenzlauer station with the pram; then he left Clara to watch them and came back for Gerda and me. The train was crowded with workers coming off the night shift. They looked dead tired and some of them were asleep. The Frankfurter Allee station was the fourth stop. We carried the suitcases and the pram downstairs. It was quite a little way to the siding where the transport was waiting but a man helped us and we did it in one trip. There was a crowd of people round the train and Hitler Youth loading the baggage. We folded up the pram and saw our things into the van. We were late and the train was already full. We could only find seats in the carriage with the N.S.V. nurse. The N.S.V. was like the W.V.S. in England. In our carriage was another mother and her little girl, Eva. With them was Helga, a classmate of Clara's. Her mother had asked us to keep an eye on her. At the last minute another girl was brought to the transport by her aunt. She put her into the carriage and explained to Eva's mother and me that her parents were divorced and that she wasn't quite right in the head, poor little Waltraut. Her aunt had got her very clean and smart for the transport. We each had to bring a plate, a cup and a knife and fork; she had a large china plate with roses on it. Willi had to go to work. We watched him climb up to the Ringbahn station. There was an alarm but it was soon over and at about eleven the train rumbled off slowly. It was an old train and the doors weren't very safe so we tied them up with string.

Of course the children quite enjoyed it. I had taken cards to play on the journey, our copy of Grimm's fairy tales and pencils and paper. We also had sandwiches and a thermos flask with coffee. Food was provided on the transport and the N.S.V. nurse was in charge of distributing it. Eva's mother said that she saw her take half-a-pound of butter and hide it in her bag. I didn't see it. I liked Eva's mother. She was a quiet decent sort of person. Her husband had a little shop.

The transport went on all day and through the night. We put the bigger children to sleep on the luggage racks. Poor little Waltraut, the one who wasn't right in the head, had no blanket so I gave her mine. As the dawn drew near I was terribly cold; she was sleeping soundly and I took it back. Over the Vistula we went. We were not supposed to raise the blind and look at it, but I did. The train rumbled over that great silver river that will last long after the Nazis and their insane crimes have been forgotten.

I was completely exhausted although we had been given every help possible: special dockets for boots for the children, coffee and food rations served during the journey. I thought of the Jews in their transports when often their carefully-packed baggage was taken from them. The story was that as they went through the barrier, to get into the cattle trucks, they had to hold their hands above their heads and leave their suitcases standing.

Morning came and we were at Koenigsberg. From there the train went to Brittanian. By this time I was pretty superstitious and was looking for lucky numbers and omens, so I thought the name was a good omen. We had to change trains and get onto a narrow gauge railway. Eva's mother, the little girls, and my family stayed together. My back was very painful and it ached terribly. I suppose it was nerves really.

It must have been about three in the afternoon when we arrived at Kuckernese. This was the terminus for the narrow gauge train. We unloaded and went to the town hall. Clara was very upset because one of the wheels had come off the pram, but I fixed it back again. We sat in the town hall and the Kuckernese housewives came and picked the evacuees they thought would suit them. Eva's mother, Eva, Helga, Waltraut and my family sat together, but Eva's mother and I decided that we would neither of us take on Waltraut. We felt badly about it, but conditions were so uncertain that we didn't want to take on extra responsibility. We sat there for a while, and then Waltraut was taken by a woman. She was a pretty little thing, and apart from a slightly vacant look, you wouldn't have known there was anything wrong with her. Not surprisingly, she wet her bed the first night and her welcome was over. Later she was moved to a farm outside the village where there were lots of children and animals but I believe she got on alright. We sat on in the town hall and then two large East Prussian women approached us. One of them wanted a mother with one child, and the other a mother with three children, and so I decided to take Helga with us.

We went out of the town hall with our pram and walked through the village with Frau Dregenus and Frau Witt. They were big women and they talked very loudly. Frau Dregenus and Frau Witt lived in modern villas outside the village. Frau Witt owned the garage and Frau Dregenus's father owned the general store which sold haberdashery and hardware. Kuckernese was a big village. It had grown up as a smuggling centre because it is on the Neman River. In the olden days before the First World War it was the boundary with Russia. There was a great smuggling trade of cheap German manufactured goods to Russia, and cheap Russian agricultural produce to Germany.

Frau Witt's house came first and then a little further along the road, across a field, was Frau Dregenus's. Her children came running out to meet us; she had six. She took us into the kitchen, a light square room, and she bade us sit down and have some potato soup. I was amazed. The kitchen was wildly untidy, and the two serving girls were bare footed. After we had eaten Frau Dregenus called one of the maids; "Laurie, my cigarettes"; she gave me one and I thought, the woman smokes, thank goodness. She sat puffing away. She was a big jolly, blonde woman with goitre. She had fallen in love and married a Lithuanian who worked in her father's shop. He was a drunkard, and the heavy drinking was probably responsible for the eldest child being a half wit. At least that is what she thought. The old grandfather who lived with them was deaf and dumb. She was kind hearted. I told her at once that I was English. In a way our skeletons in the cupboard cancelled out: one being English and the other having a mentally-deficient child. In Germany that was a sort of crime and there was a law about sterilisation of the unfit but nobody knew exactly who was unfit. After lunch and our cigarettes she took me upstairs and showed me the rooms we were to have. There were two and a little kitchen. Also she gave me an electric cooking pot as the stove burned wood or coal. She told me that our rooms were terribly cold in the winter and that the potatoes that were stored there the year before had frozen. I scrubbed the floors and, even on that summer's day, they took a long time to dry. But I had a stove and I had a kitchen. I felt this is alright and as I unpacked, the pain in my back gradually eased off. It was a relief as in Berlin we always had to keep the suitcases half-packed because of the raids. You never knew from one day to the next whether you would have a home.

I had a pound of lump sugar which we had taken for the journey. The

Dregenus children had come to watch me unpack and I gave them lumps of sugar. She gave my children apples from her apple tree. When I had unpacked, I took the children and we went round to Eva's mother at Frau Witt's house. Eva's mother had to share the kitchen with Frau Witt. The latter was over bearing and she came to dislike her very much. We all went for a walk along the levee at the side of the river. The Neman is a lovely river but it overflows when the ice breaks in the spring. On either side there is a great earth wall and behind this bank are the farmhouses. On every farmhouse roof is a stork's nest and on every nest a stork, standing on one leg. We walked along in the fresh air, sun and wind and thanked providence for putting us in such a beautiful land.

Mid-day meals were provided for the evacuees in the town hall but the children didn't like them. As soon as I could get coal, I started cooking on my stove. We got coal almost at once because in the village there was a sort of aristocracy of shop people. Potatoes were no problem; Frau Dregenus organised a sack from a farmer. The bread ration was better than in Berlin. The baker didn't bother too much about exact portions and the bread was much better. Fats and meats were the same and once a week you could get black pudding. The water it was boiled in had a lot of fat. We used to get this in Berlin too. The fat in the water was about four times the fat allowed on your ration card. The children were very hungry. They ate two or three big potatoes for their dinner and four or five slices of bread for their tea. For supper, Frau Dregenus let me cook on her electric stove in her kitchen. We always had a milk soup.

One of the teachers, Frau Kopp, organised a sewing evening for the Berlin mothers. We were allowed to use the board room of the bank. It was on the first floor and had central heating, so it was lovely and warm. We did the mending for the children whose mothers weren't with them. The first evening Frau Kopp read aloud to us. She read rather well. She was from East Prussia herself and chose some rather gloomy Lithuanian stories full of storms and tragedy. I enjoyed them but most of the mothers didn't. They had enough troubles of their own with husbands at the front. Many of them had never been out of Berlin in their lives and were very homesick. They didn't like the country and the sad Lithuanian tales made them feel even more miserable. We finished about ten o'clock and started for home. It was absolutely pitch dark. You could only find your way along the street by feeling the edge of the pavement with your feet. I had the furthest to go and as I got out of the village I could just see my way by the sky being a fraction lighter between the tops of the trees on either side of the road. It was rather exciting but I was glad when I saw the light in Frau Witt's house and then further on in ours. I got in and made myself some coffee.

I liked Frau Dregenus and she really was very good to us. We had to get supplies of vegetables in for the winter, carrots, cabbages and potatoes. She let us store them in her cellar which was under the kitchen. In return I tried to help her as much as I could. In Kuckernese there was no vegetable or fruit shop so people got their supplies from the farmers, or grew their own. Later in the winter they did open a shop for the Berlin mothers. I tried to teach Inge, the mentally handicapped child, to read, but of course I couldn't. Once a week we gave the children a bath. There was a bathroom next to the kitchen. The water was heated with a stove in which she used to burn old cartons from her father's shop. We put all the girls in the bath first and then all the boys. One day her little boy climbed the roof and put a brick down my chimney. Between us we cleaned the chimney and, although it made a terrible mess, I think we both rather enjoyed it. At Christmas time she roasted two geese in order that she could bottle them for the spring. The electricity was always cutting out because the overhead wiring broke down if it was stormy, or there was too much snow. So she cooked the geese in my little wood burning oven upstairs. We spent practically the whole of one night doing this as you had to keep replenishing the wood to keep the oven hot enough.

We adopted a stray cat but I found it had a tapeworm and I was afraid the children might catch it. I decided that I must destroy the cat. I did it myself because I thought if I gave it to the boys they would do it cruelly. I found a sack and a stone and drowned it. It's an awful thing to do; to feel the life going out of an animal. Another horrific thing was a fire at one of the neighbouring farms. The fire brigade, such as it was, was too slow to stop it. Everybody from the village went to watch. The roaring and crackling of the flames and the crashing of the beams made more impression on me than all the destruction and burning in the Berlin raids. There were a lot of pigs in the farm. They were all roasted in the fire and laid out on the grass afterwards.

Clara had tonsillitis. She wasn't very bad but I had to keep her in bed. Helga was homesick and wanted to stay in bed too. The doctor, who was young and rather good, told me to let her. I'm afraid I slightly resented having to nurse her as well, as there was nothing really wrong with her. I realised he was right; they both got better after two or three days. Helga had wonderful hair; she could nearly sit on it. However washing it was a job. Clara used to do it for her. When we arrived Helga wrote to her mother. In English fashion, I didn't read the letter as I didn't want her to feel that there was any censorship. Her mother wrote back, enclosing the letter, and pointing out the spelling and grammar mistakes, asking me in future to correct the letters. So much for German attitudes. Helga was a bed wetter; her mother had told me this. She was terribly good about it, trying to get up in time. I used to lift her late at night and we managed pretty well. She was an easy child to get on with, and after her initial homesickness, I think she was happy. She had a splendid appetite. I had managed to scrounge vitamin C tablets. I found myself resenting giving Helga the same as my own children, but naturally she wanted the same as the others. Her mother sent me sweets and cigarettes and I was able to give Frau Dregenus some which did help the general atmosphere. Her mother came and fetched her before the winter really started. She was a nice young woman and she found a place for Helga much nearer Berlin, where she could visit her. I was glad not to have the responsibility as one never knew what was coming.

I rather liked doing the washing. We boiled it on the electric stove in Frau Dregenus's kitchen in a zinc pan. Then we took it out into the yard and washed it in a big tub and rinsed it, then up on the line, big sheets drying in the wind. In the winter we hung them up in an empty room upstairs where they took a week to dry.

The Berliner children had their own teachers. School was in shifts. On alternate weeks the village children had morning school and the next week it was the other way round. One of the Berlin teachers, Herr Gross, organised a choir of the mothers. We practised in the room over the bank where we had our sewing evenings. We used to sing in the church. It was a bare North German Lutheran church with plain windows. We sat and sang up in the gallery. In the spring, when the children from Kuckernese and the surrounding farms were confirmed, we sang Bach's Jubilate. It was a very moving service with the girls in their white dresses and the boys in their first proper suits. I enjoyed the singing.

On the road to the village was a farm where the children used to go and play. It was a big farm and had a great barn where all the animals were kept in the winter. They had beautiful tall East Prussian horses and they had Polish slave workers who also lived in the barn. Sometimes, in the evening, we heard them singing Polish songs. They had absolutely nothing but rags for clothing. Frau Dregenus had a sewing machine which she let me use. I made a coat for Clara out of an old one of mine. One of the mothers, who was a dressmaker, helped me. I also made a dress for one of the Polish slave workers at the farm. One of the teachers, who I thought was rather nice, was absolutely horrified that I did this. She said, "But aren't you afraid that they will murder you?" I thought this fantastic. She was a good teacher and seemed intelligent, and yet she also believed this absurd nonsense about 'unter menschen'. Frau Dregenus, Frau Witt, and the coal merchant's wife used to play cards once a week. They took it in turns to go to each other's houses. They played a game called 'bubengraben'. It was fairly complicated, a little like sixty-six for four hands. They gambled for low stakes. She invited me to make a fourth when it was our house and I did once or twice. I gave it up because I couldn't sit and listen to their remarks about Jews and Poles, let alone the British. Frau Witt, who was a pretty nasty piece of work, would make provocative remarks. Once I remember them commenting about an air raid in Berlin, which had killed a lot of Polish slave workers who lived in barracks near Siemens. They said it was a jolly good thing. Once I was walking with them to the village and we met a Pole who asked the way. They questioned him, what he was doing, where he was coming from, and where he was going. Afterwards they said they ought to let the police know. I got them talking about something else and they forgot the Pole.

I stayed upstairs in my little kitchen and read. I borrowed Schiller's history of the Thirty Years War. It shone with integrity and brilliance against the background of Nazi Germany with its obscene obscurantism. I also read The Merchant of Venice and the power and passion of Shylock's defence really came over to me.

The autumn came and Frau Dregenus moved us into a different room over the kitchen. It had a big white china stove which took up nearly a quarter of the room. It faced south so we got some sun. She was afraid we would be too cold in the other room, which faced north. We had coal because of Frau Dregenus's friendship with the coal merchant's wife. Fortunately it wasn't a very cold winter. I think we never had more than twenty degrees of frost. Sometimes, when it eased up and we only had about six or seven degrees, it felt quite warm. However the snow lasted till the beginning of May. All the time the Russians were advancing and one mother after another got the news that their husbands were either fallen or missing. One mother was terribly worried because she had no black stockings to wear for the mourning. I wondered when our turn would come. Willi had visited us twice, once in late summer and once at Christmas time. That time he told me he had an escaped prisoner living in our flat in the Gubitzstrasse. It happened like this. We had a friend, a comrade, called Yonny. Yonny had a lover called Alf who was from Hamburg. At the beginning of Nazi times he was arrested for being a communist but he escaped to Holland. Yonny, who was passionately in love with Alf, went to Holland and persuaded him to come back to Germany illegally, promising she would look after him. Alf came back, partly because we all of us believed that the Nazis would be overthrown, and partly because the refugees in Holland led a bitter life scraping a living and never belonging anywhere. Alf lived in Germany illegally right through the whole period until the autumn of 1943 when he was arrested and imprisoned in Ploetzensee Prison. Just before Christmas there was a very heavy raid and the prison was badly bombed. Alf could have escaped but he didn't because it would have been impossible for him to live anywhere. In the prison he had met an old friend from Hamburg called Ernst Bästlein who was condemned to death. Ernst escaped and went to Yonny who sent him to Willi.

They had organised food. Some friends had a small machine tool factory and they could get food on the black market. Will was very excited about this and he felt he was doing something at last. He had a sort of hero worship for Ernst Bästlein. I wasn't so sure about it. Not about helping Ernst to escape, but Willi also said they were going to organise resistance and get weapons. It seemed to me the best thing we could do was to stay alive. Germany had lost the war. It was only a question of time, and then everybody would be needed to reorganise a different sort of Germany. I thought it was romantic at this stage to think you could do anything inside Germany to break the Nazi hold but I could see for Willi it was absolutely necessary to act. Also I thought perhaps I was wrong and just rationalising my cowardice.

Willi went back to Berlin. We were warm in our room, but very often the lights didn't work. There was nothing for it but to go to bed and tell the children fairy stories. I knew a lot of Grimm's Fairy Stories by heart. It gave one an idea of what it must have been like in olden times in the long, dark winter evenings and how big a part the story telling must have played.

Two boys, Berliners, fell one day through the ice when they were sliding on a pond. One of the mothers, with great presence of mind, lay down on the ice and managed to pull one of them out, but the other one died. It turned out that he had a weak heart and died from shock when he fell into the cold water.

Everyone was very proud of the brave mother and there was a special presentation to her. Fraulein Kopp, the one who read the Lithuanian stories on the first sewing evening, tried hard to get the mothers to enjoy the countryside. She took us for walks in the evening along the levee to hear the nightingales and when the river was covered with ice she led us dangerously out onto it; actually I fell in, but not very far. On one of the nightingale walks she confided to me that she was engaged to be married. She showed me the photograph of her young man. He looked very handsome and a bit young for her, she was about forty, but it never occurred to me that she was making it up. She asked me if I thought it would be good idea to tell the mothers as it would be something to take their minds off their troubles. It seemed quite a good idea to me if she didn't mind herself. She took another mother, Frau Konniscienski, into her confidence, and between the two of us everybody soon knew about it. One of the teachers organised an engagement present, an art book, which we were to give her when the engagement was to be formally announced. It was a dud art book because under Hitler all art was forbidden except classical stuff, and it had to be German. This would have meant Cranach, Grunewald and Durer, which the mothers wouldn't have liked. So it was what corresponds to English nineteenth century, really terrible, but it was expensively got up and the mothers liked it. The great day came. Herr Gross had rehearsed the choir. We sang, 'Horch, Wer kommt von draussen rein' and 'Sie hat zwei blaue Augen' and 'Guten Abend gute Nacht', which I couldn't stand because they always dragged it. All was ready, but unfortunately the young man couldn't be there. This didn't surprise anybody very much and we carried on singing and made the presentation. Later it turned out that the whole thing was a fake. The photo was a film star. Whether she believed it herself, I don't know, but the mothers were angry because of the money they had given for the art book. This came out after I had gone back to Berlin.

Willi came at the end of May and we went to Nidden on the Kurische

Nehrung for a fortnight's holiday. We took the steamer from Kuckernese. We had to be there early, about six o'clock in the morning. We pushed the pram through Kuckernese. The sun had just risen and the shadows of the trees made diagonal stripes across the straight road that led down to the river. On the steamer were a group of 'Arbeitdienst Mädel'[1] in their blue linen dresses and embroidered aprons. They sang folk songs as the steamer puffed its way down the river to the Nehrung. They were going for a day's outing to the sea. We stayed in a little hotel in Nidden and went for walks across the dunes to the Baltic strand, silver and lonely by the blue sea. It was hot, and the little pine trees and the flowers on the sandy dunes smelt sweet.

The fortnight came to an end and Willi went back. He took the steamer to Tilsit and from there the night train to Berlin. I stayed on another day or two before going back to Kuckernese.

The next day, when we came in from the beach for lunch, we heard the news that the Allies had landed in Normandy. It was D-Day.

1 young working girls

Chapter 4 Berlin 1944

I suppose I was pretty sure that something was wrong. Then I received a hundred marks from Willi but there was no letter with it. I thought to myself, it's alright, the letter will come tomorrow; perhaps he hasn't had time to write, or the letter got lost, but still no letter came. Then a telegram came. It was unsigned. It said, 'Direct hit, return to Berlin at once'. I still managed to hope that it was just a raid and our house had been bombed. I rang his firm where he worked and they told me that he had been arrested the day he got back from Kuckernese. He had never been back to work. I panicked. This thing had been hanging over our heads for so long that, when it did come, I lost my nerve. I didn't want to take the children back to Berlin. It had become a sort of nightmare place for me. I telegraphed Oma in Bremen to try to get her to come to East Prussia and look after the children while I went to Berlin. I was in a terrible state. I didn't want to leave the children. I didn't know how quickly Germany would break up, or how soon the Russians would advance. Oma telegraphed back and told me to come to Bremen. I took Fraulein Kopp into my confidence. I think Frau Dregenus must have realised what had happened although I pretended that we had been bombed. Anyway, I took the children to Bremen. It was a nightmare journey. Fraulein Kopp and one or two of the mothers helped us push the pram with our belongings to the Kuckernese station. We had to wait at Koenigsberg for a couple of hours and we went into the town. It had not been bombed at all. I remember being very shocked at seeing a woman refuse to give her seat to a wounded soldier. Perhaps she was ill, but I just thought Germans don't even care about their own people; they are just mean all through. Of course we had to go by Berlin, but I didn't go home. The Ringbahn train went past our street and we could see our house. We reached Bremen and I stayed one night there. There was a raid and I watched poor Oma getting dressed with her hands shaking. We went to their shelter which was a tunnel under the railway. The ends had been blocked with concrete barriers and sand bags. Everybody knew one another. I think it must have been more like the atmosphere in the air raid shelters in England.

I discussed the whole thing with Mieke and Klarchen. It was a relief

Willi's passport photo, probably taken in 1943. The passport contained a visa for Norway. His firm Bamag A.G. were involved with the heavy water project in Norway

to talk openly with them, but I had lost my nerve, and in a way I was playing the part of a heroine. I left the children in Bremen and went back to Berlin. I felt terrible on the train. I had to talk to people, and this is where I don't know how much was imagined and how much was real. On the train I talked to a man who seemed kind. I must have told him about my home being bombed or something like that. It seemed to me that he knew more about it than an ordinary stranger. He said "Go straight home. Do not visit anybody before you reach home." It was good advice, and I would have done well to follow it but I just couldn't bear the thought of our flat in the Gubitzstrasse. Instead I got out of the train at an earlier station and went to the Havel. Yonny and Alf had their boat there and I thought Yonny might be there. I desperately needed to talk to somebody and I thought Yonny might have some idea of what had happened. It was a peaceful grey evening when I reached the lakeside and the boat was there. I walked across the gang plank and down the steps into the cabin. Yonny was lying on the bunk in the cabin almost as if she was waiting for me. I sometimes think now that perhaps she was. Could she have been the one to betray us? She was madly in love with Alf. He only got a four-year sentence and afterwards, when she was in prison, she received a special diet due to her kidney disease.

But at that time no such thoughts occurred to me and I was so thankful to find her. She gave me peppermint tea and food. She told me that it was Vera who sent me the telegram. We talked the whole thing over and Yonny didn't know much about it. She thought the best thing was to go and see Vera and Lucy. I had meant to go home that evening but I was so tired and it was so comforting to be with Yonny on the boat that I stayed the night. I decided to go and see Vera before I went home. If I was questioned I would pretend that I didn't know them and say that I had arrived in Berlin a day later. In the morning I went to Vera who lived in Zehlendorf and found her and Lucy. They were thankful that I had come as I was the only one who could go to the Gestapo and try to find out what had happened. All Vera knew was that Willi had arranged to telephone when he got back from his holiday. He didn't telephone so she went to the Gubitzstrasse but nobody answered the door. While she was standing there a neighbour, probably Frau Zuhlke, told her that the Gestapo had arrested Willi. Then she sent me the telegram. They gave me strawberries; it was about the only thing I could have eaten. We thought the best thing was to go home and then go and see the Gestapo.

We arranged to meet at Ostkreuz the next day at six in the evening. I was to telephone if I couldn't make it.

So I went home to the Gubitzstrasse. It was grim and the flat was dusty. Willi and Ernst had muffled the gas meter, which was directly by the door, with paper and blankets. The meter made a loud ticking noise and they were afraid that, if Ernst did some cooking during the day when Willi was at work, the neighbours would hear. On the table in Willi's room were three dirty cups. The Gestapo had taken our wireless set.

I found one of the neighbours, Frau Schroer, at home. She told me that the Gestapo had waited in the flat for three days. Willi left us on the Saturday and he should have arrived home on the Sunday but he didn't get to the flat until the Wednesday. What was he doing in those three days? Did he realise something was wrong and try to escape from Germany? He had a Norwegian visa in his passport because his firm, Bamag A.G., was going to send him there. The firm made apparatus used on the Eastern Front to cut up the metal of guns which couldn't otherwise be moved, or something like that. The Norway trip had to do with the heavy water project for the German atom bomb. Willi was to go there to work as a draughtsman. He intended to escape to Sweden and somehow get to England. Be that as it may, it is possible that the Gestapo waited for me to come back to Berlin before they arrested Vera to see if I was in contact with allied espionage about this. This would explain why they took so little interest in me afterwards. You can imagine, and imagine, and imagine. At that time we had no knowledge that such a thing as an atom bomb existed.

There was nothing to eat in the flat except peppermint tea, but I don't think I couldn't have eaten anything anyway. The next morning there was a fairly bad air raid. I went with Frau Schroer to the shelter. It was about ten minutes away on the ring road towards Weissensee. It had been built by Polish slave labour in about 1941 and was below ground with reinforced concrete walls and roof. It was packed with people, all very hysterical, and it gave me a claustrophobic feeling. I thought, if there was a direct hit and the ventilation gave out, it would be a most unpleasant death. I preferred to take a chance in our cellar. The raid finished about midday.

I went first to the Bamag office to find out what I could from them. They had been bombed out of their factory in the Pulitzstrasse but were in a house not far away. I came out of the station, I think it was the

Tiergartenstrasse, and walked down the street. I walked through those ruined streets, long perspectives of empty walls with the window holes staring down, and every hundred yards or so a great mass of rubble where a house had a direct hit. I found the firm up some stairs in a house that still had a roof. In the office they were very kind. They gave me a paper which Willi had to sign. It was a claim for compensation for his slide rule and an overall which were burnt when they were bombed out. This was useful because if I could get his signature I would know he was alive. They also rang up the Gestapo for me and made an appointment. Then I went to the Gestapo which was in a large building near Oranianburger Tor. A very young S.S. man was standing guard at the gate. The porter came out and took me upstairs. The building seemed empty, yet full of agony of those who had been questioned there. Upstairs I found a rather bare and messy office with two Gestapo men in it. One of them was the Herr Schmidt I had been told to see. I said that I was the wife of Willi Jungmittag and had a form from the firm which he must sign to get some money that was due to him. There was an empty chair so I sat down on it and pretended to take the whole thing calmly. The Gestapo man telephoned and said if I went to Prinz Albrechtstrasse I could get my husband to sign the form but that I couldn't see him. I stood up to go and he said, "Where is your entrance permit?" I said I hadn't got one. There was a woman secretary who came in while I was talking. She turned round and hissed viciously "We'll see how you get out then." I kept calm and said if the man downstairs hadn't given me a permit it wasn't my fault and they had better do something about it. Herr Schmidt said "Well come on then", and he took me downstairs through a different door. When we reached the S.S. man at the gate, he went for him and asked why he hadn't given me a permit. The man, he was hardly more than a boy, answered that it was because the porter had taken me up, which was true. Herr Schmidt threatened him that if it ever happened again he'd finish him. The S.S. man went as white as a sheet. I can still see his white face with its expression of terror against the dark doorway.

I was pleased with myself. I'd found out where Willi was and I hadn't been frightened by the Gestapo. The Prinz Albrechtstrasse had a reputation for being one of the worst S.S. prisons for torture. I had to go about four stations on the underground. It was near the Potsdammer Platz. In the olden days I had been to student dances there. I think it used to be the Architecture Faculty of the Berlin University. But conditions had changed, so although I knew it well, no memories were awakened. I didn't recognise it as the same place although I could see it was. I was allowed in and this time I was given a chit with the time on it. I get the same sort of chit nowadays when I go to the German Embassy in London to collect my German compensation money. I had to go through the building and down some stairs to the prison. There was a door and a bell. I rang it and a man opened a little grill in the door. I told him what I wanted and he took the compensation form for the slide rule and overalls. I waited about ten minutes. I sat on the stairs and read the paper. Everything in me resented this standing and the imploring attitude that they expected you to take up. As I sat there, I saw a notice on the door saying that relations were allowed to bring food and clean clothes for the prisoners. The grill was opened and I was given the paper back. It was signed but the handwriting was very shaky. I went home and collected some food: strawberries from the allotment, a bottle of fruit juice and some clothes. I didn't have any other food. I went again into the prison, down the stairs and rang the bell. The grill opened again and the man told me I would need special permission from the Oranianburger from Herr Schmidt. So I took the U-bahn back again, but when I got there I was told that Herr Schmidt had gone home and there was nobody there. There was a telephone box just across the road and I thought I could slip in and give Vera a ring. I got into the box and started to dial when a man came into the box. Somehow I couldn't stop dialling until I had done five of the numbers. The man said he was from Vienna and was not sure how to work the Berlin telephone. It was obvious that he was watching me. I went out of the telephone booth dazed. The shock of it staggered me and lamed my brain. I had arranged to meet Vera at Ostkreuz at six o'clock. It was about four thirty and I thought I had time to escape my followers. I went from one train to another but it was obvious that I was too slow so I went home beaten. I went upstairs to my flat and tried to pull myself together. I made some herb tea but I had no sugar and it didn't help much. They had five out of the six digits of Vera's telephone number. I had to warn her somehow to cut off all communication with the organisation. I didn't undress that night because I thought they would be coming for me at any moment. I decided to get up before it was light, put on Willi's Macintosh, and go down through the back of the gardens where there was a hole in the wall due to the bombing. I could walk to a tram stop and go and see Vera. And that is what I did. I thought all was clear, and then I thought that perhaps someone was watching me, but I just couldn't stop myself. I reached Vera's flat and rang the bell. There was no answer so I rang next door as I knew they were friends. The woman came to the door and she looked terrified. She said that all the Glass family had been arrested the evening before and told me to go to hell. I was absolutely dazed and thought it was all my fault; also that they would come for me, as I was obviously an accomplice. I stayed in Berlin for a week waiting to be arrested. The air raids continued all the time but I didn't go to the shelter or bother to go to the cellar. I remember looking out of the window one night and seeing the sky all lit up with search lights and the red glow of the fires behind the houses. It was extraordinarily beautiful and fantastic, something like the last judgement.

I waited for a week and then got in touch with a lawyer Yonny had advised me to go to, but he was too afraid to take the case, I think because I was English. I went back to Bremen, collected the children, and came home. By this time I couldn't sit down in a room or keep still, but I had to try and keep a normal life for the children. There was no school so I had them on my hands the whole day. A good many other people had come back to Berlin because they were afraid of the Russians, and some of Clara's school friends were among them. Gerda, who was nearly four, played in the streets all day. It wasn't dangerous because there were no cars. Clara had roller skates and went skating with her friends in the streets. We also went bathing in the Jungfernheide Lake at Siemenstadt but it was risky because of the raids. All round the lake the trees were blasted and dead but it were something to do. My neighbours were pretty good to me but they were frightened to have a lot to do with me. We went to the air raid shelter all together. There were about three raids a day. Actually I found the raids a relief as they took my mind off the other thing. I went every week to the Prinz Albrechtstrasse prison with clean clothes for Willi and took the dirty washing home to wash. I didn't dare to contact Yonny in case I put the Gestapo on her track.

Finally I decided to try and get evacuated again. I wanted to escape from Berlin and the raids. I was afraid that some comrade might visit me and I was sure I was being watched. Now, I think it was persecution mania. I hadn't much money and if I was evacuated I could get money

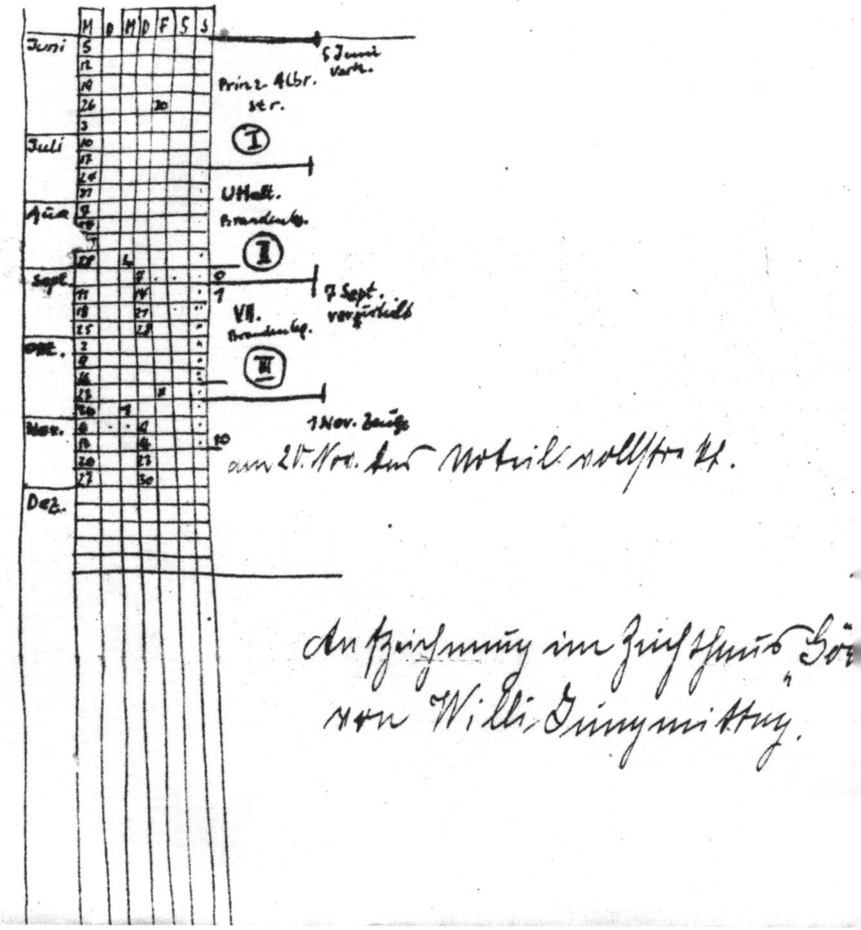

This is the calendar that Willi made in prison. He was arrested June 5th 1944 and sent to Prinz Albrecht Str. prison. It was well known for beatings and torture. About six weeks later in July he was transferred to Brandenburg prison. On the 7th September he was sentenced to death and executed (guillotined) on November 20th 1944.

from the state.

Then one Friday I went to the prison. It was the day after the attempt on Hitler's life and there were double guards at the door. An S.S. man accompanied me through the building and down the stairs to the prison. They said that my husband was not there and they didn't know where he was. I was told to go to the Orianburger and ask. I did this and met with the same reply. I wondered if they had just bumped the lot off. Then I thought up the excuse that I had to let the room in the flat and I needed Will's keys. The Orianburger office told me to go to the Gestapo headquarters at Potsdam.

It was a Saturday afternoon. I left the children with Frau Zuhlke and took the train to Potsdam. I realised I was going to be questioned. All the way on the train I hammered out in my head what I was going to say. I mustn't say that I had been to see Vera and Yonny. When I arrived I was let in and the door locked behind me. I was too frightened already for this to make any difference. I went up to the Gestapo office. There were three men there; they seemed to be higher up Gestapo officials. They told me to sit down and asked me how I had come to know that Willi was arrested. I said that I had no news from him and I had telephoned his firm. I knew that I mustn't mention Vera's telegram. I was so scared that I could only bring the words out slowly. They didn't pursue this but asked if I knew Yonny. I said I did. We had arranged this long before, to say that she had taken English lessons from me. Did I know Alf? Had I ever been to their flat? Yes, once. I said I didn't know Alf but I had met Yonny's boyfriend and I thought he was called Alf. They let me go. I think I must have made such a dumb impression that they really thought I didn't know anything about it. With the Gestapo in Orianburger I had always told the same story. I knew nothing of Willi's political doings but that he had got into bad company while I was evacuated and that he had been led into the whole thing by loneliness and was really a good German. What else was there to say? Heroics would not have done any good and would have finished me off as well. I went home again and a few days later received a letter from Willi. He was in Brandenburg Prison and it was much better than the Prinz Albrechtstrasse. There was no beating up in the prison; he wrote 'ohne qualerei'.[1] I was thankful. I hoped the war would end in time to save his life.

1 no torture

I decided to try and get the children away from Berlin. I was in touch with a lawyer, who had been given the job of defending Willi by the Gestapo, but he was no use. I didn't know of any other lawyer and was afraid to get in touch with other comrades for fear of endangering them. I hoped the war would come to an end before Willi's case came up for trial. The Gestapo man told me it would take some months before they collected the evidence. It was now September 1944. I was refused evacuation. I had got to the point of having all my papers ready. I had been down to the food office to change the ration cards and went to get the tickets. They told us to wait. Everybody else was fixed up and still I waited. Then I was told the Gestapo had telephoned through and I could not be evacuated. I was bitterly disappointed. I had everything packed and ready and hoped that getting away from Berlin would enable me to pull myself together. A few days later I met our estate agent in the road. He told me that my husband had been condemned to death the day before. Neither the lawyer nor the Gestapo had let me know and I could have been at the trial. The only comfort was that Vera, Lucy and Herr Glass had each received a two year sentence. Thank God that my stupid behaviour had not sentenced them to death. To Willi it had made no difference. I went at once to see the lawyer. I had to wait for two hours or so; he was a dusty little man. He showed me the files of people he had been defending with one death sentence after another. He told me that I should be allowed to see my husband and that I could put in a plea for mercy. I obtained permission to see my husband and went to Brandenburg.

I went to the prison. To get there I had to go to the Potsdam station. At the front of the train was a prison coach. The prisoners who were going there were all standing on the station handcuffed together, older men in dusty clothes with a look of complete desperation in their exhausted grey faces. There were some women, slave workers I think. The train jogged through the pleasant Brandenburg landscape; it was like a summer's day. At the station one took a tram to the prison which was on the outskirts of the town. It was a huge modern prison. It looked like a cinema prison. One went through the gates and waited in a little side room with a table and some chairs. All the time there was a regular sort of clanking noise; I don't know what it could have been. Then a warder came and I went with him through the prison. It was sunny and the grey walls were white in the sunlight. We came to a building and went in. The room was divided by a sort of wooden barrier with what looked like pews on each side. Willi came in on the other side. He didn't look so bad but the meeting was an ordeal. I had to pretend that we were quite O.K. that we were going to be evacuated again and that the raids weren't too bad. He had to keep up his side of it. We didn't dare to say anything to give ourselves away. In the end he voluntarily stopped the interview. I think we both had the impression that they would let us talk over the time allotted, hoping for some information. I was sure that other people, besides the warders, were listening. This may just have been my persecution mania. I came out into the sunlight and in a way I envied Willi because he didn't have to cope.

I decided to try and get the children evacuated even if I couldn't go myself. I was afraid the raids might get worse and I wanted to give them a chance to live. I didn't believe that I would survive. We would all have been caught and exterminated, one by one. Fraulein Zhulke, the sister-in-law of our neighbours, was going with a transport of children to Saxony and she arranged for Clara to go with them. Clara was very fond of her and wanted to go. I had told her that I didn't think there was much chance of survival in Berlin. The day she went I was in a terrible state. I kept on begging her not to go, a terrible thing to do to a child, but I was really out of my mind at the time. We had the book Huckleberry Finn from the library and I read it to the children. It made me feel better and took my mind away from the awful thoughts in my head. I took her to the train with Gerda and we saw her off. She was quite happy with Fraulein Zhulke and made friends with the other little girls. I had managed to buy her some new stockings, those German white knee socks. When Gerda and I got home I felt so completely desolate. A few days earlier I had broken our only good knife trying to get a carrot out of the hard ground in our allotment; it snapped off. I had to talk with somebody and went down to the flat below. Herr Zuhlke was alone; his wife had gone to stay with relations outside Berlin. He suggested it would help if I slept with him. I thought it might; I knew I was in the middle of a nervous breakdown. I tried giving myself electric shocks. Also I needed human contact of some sort. It did make me sleep because up to that time I couldn't. Otherwise it made things worse. At first I thought I was pregnant because I stopped menstruating but this was just shock. I didn't know that under great stress it was quite common for people to copulate. I waited till Gerda had gone to sleep and went down to the flat below.

I made an appeal for mercy for Willi. His parents, Oma and Opa did the same. Oma came from Bremen and we went together to the Brandenburg prison. It was a beautiful autumn day. We saw Willi in a different room in the prison. We were allowed to embrace and sat together. He looked much more haggard and told us he was chained all the time except for the interview. Oma had the presence of mind to bring some apples from Bremen. He ate them as we talked. We said good-bye. From the prison Oma and I walked two or three tram stops through the lovely forest in the sunshine together. I was glad he had been able to see his mother; she was more use to him than I was. I was too stunned to be much use.

The letter came telling me that Willi had been executed (guillotined) on the 20th November and enclosed his last letter. He said that in the Brandenburg Prison everything was orderly without 'quälerei'[1] and that he would get a cigarette before he was executed. He begged me to see that the children received a good education.

The winter went on. There was no heating at all. We had potatoes because I was lucky with my sack and had good ones. We did have rations of bread, fat and meat, but by this time it was very little. I couldn't bear to send Gerda away. She played on the streets. She had a friend called Carola who had a dog and who lived in the flats opposite. These were built just before the war. I received a very unhappy letter from Clara and applied for a permit to visit her and to my surprise I got one. You couldn't travel without a permit. Clara was in Saxony at a place called Sohland am Spree. In the end the children's transport had been divided and Clara was not with Fraulein Zhulke. She cried for the first fortnight and then settled down. By the time we got there she was better. She and another little girl were quartered with an old woman who had a little shop in the village. They slept upstairs in the attic room. There was no heating but the children had good feather beds. There was nowhere in the village for Gerda and me to stay so we slept on Clara's bed, and Clara slept with the other little girl. We stayed two nights. Fortunately it was fine sunny weather. There was snow on the ground and we went for a walk in a valley in the forest. I didn't tell Clara about her father; I just said he was at the war. I couldn't make up my mind

1 torture

whether to take her back with me. I wanted her but I was afraid of the air raids. I still thought I might be arrested and that would make it worse for her. I cried and sometimes begged her to come back with us and then begged her not to. She had a big doll that she was fond of and Gerda broke it. In the end we left her on the station crying, but I believe that after we had gone she went back to her school friends and it wasn't so bad.

Our train back was very slow and it was very cold. We had to change at Dresden and we waited there in the middle of the night for two hours. This was before Dresden was bombed. Gerda had a nasty cough and wasn't well. When I got home I took her to the doctor. It was whooping cough but fortunately she didn't have it badly. Our doctor gave her injections. I had to go to the labour exchange to see if I was fit for work. We had been receiving National Assistance. We had to be stripped naked to be examined by the doctor at the labour exchange. Being a painter I had no feelings about being naked; I didn't mind, but it did seem to be rather degrading, they only sounded your heart and lungs. I was told that I would have to go and work but I couldn't do this till Gerda was over the whooping cough. This lasted five weeks until after Christmas.

Oma and Klarchen came to Berlin once more and we went on a frightful cold day to Brandenburg Prison to get Willi's things. Just after we arrived at the Brandenburg station there was a bad raid. We went into the station shelter. After the raid we took the tram to the prison and we passed a big factory that had been badly bombed, it was still smoking and burning. We were given Willi's clothes and a chart he made in prison with pin pricks for each day. On the way home we had to go to an office to get some papers stamped. I was dead tired and there was a chair in the office so I sat down on it. Oma shouted at me to get up, "Don't sit down Brigitte in front of an official." That was the trouble with Germans: this deep respect for the authorities. The next day Oma and Klarchen left us and went back to Bremen. Before she went she said to me "Putz du deine Wohnung und hast du deine Beschäftigung."[1] Of course in a way she was right. If I could have concentrated on keeping up some sort of appearance, it would probably have kept me a bit better. Not that it was actually much use, cleaning the flat without soap and with air raids every night breaking a few more bits of glass in the win-

1 Clean your flat and you'll have something to do

dows. I, being middle class, had never really learnt the routine of cleaning, so it didn't work for me as a sort of Zen activity, which it probably did for her. Actually I contemplated committing suicide while they were there by jumping off the balcony. I thought it would be better for Gerda if they took her back to Bremen with them, but I funked it.

When Gerda was over her whooping cough I found a nursery not far off and looked for a job. One wasn't directed into a job, I don't think people were, but you couldn't change jobs if you were in a war factory. I went to the labour exchange and there were two jobs, one in a restaurant washing up and the one in a factory. I chose the factory because it was very near the nursery and I could walk there. It was a light engineering firm, quite small. I'd never worked in a factory before. At first I did filing. In the beginning I was very worried because I was literally chewing my fingers and they were all sore. I was afraid the metal filings would poison the sores but to my surprise they healed them. Then I was put onto drilling but I was very bad at it and did some unintentional sabotage by breaking drills. So in the end they put me to working a hand pump for one of the machines. I had my dinner at the factory but we brought our own food. I generally had cold potatoes. There were so many electricity cuts that we didn't do much work. I didn't like working in this factory but, although the other women were slightly antagonistic because I was English and they sensed the class difference and the fact that I was terribly nervous, there was comradeship. They made jokes about what would happen when the Russians came. One or two tried to take it out on me and one or two of them were friendly. The foremen were kindly and tried to explain the work to me. Then came a very bad raid. It must have been some time in February, it was in the morning and I was at work in the little factory. We went to the shelter and sat listening to the thumps, thinking that every minute might be our last; then it died down. When the all clear went I rushed out to see what had happened to the nursery. When I got above ground the whole place seemed to be burning. I ran through the debris and got to the nursery. It was burning. I found the children in the Hitler Youth Home in the shelter there. They were all right but the Hitler Youth Home was burning too. Nobody seemed to know what to do, so I took them to our flat, which I could see was still standing, left them there with one of the nurses, and went back to try to put out the fire in the nursery. Quite a few parents had turned up and we organised a relay with buckets of water and did succeed in keeping it in check until the fire brigade came. Our factory was bombed out and the nursery was too badly damaged for the children to go any more. I stopped going to work. Nobody seemed to bother about it any more. We just sat in our cold flat and ate our potatoes which we cooked on the gas, although the pressure was so low it took about an hour to cook them.

Tom came to visit us. He was Genia's son. Genia was Jewish; her husband was Aryan, but a communist. He was arrested at the beginning of the war and died in Sachsenhausen concentration camp. Tom had heard that Willi was dead and thought I might be able to give him some clothes. Genia was transported in 1943, presumably to the gas chambers. Tom was fourteen when this happened. I had already given the clothes to the Winter Help for refugees from the east. I was frightened and wanted to give myself a good mark so I had nothing for Tom. I had a big map on the wall and I could see how the Russians were advancing. I had let Willi's room to a little hunchback woman. It must have been awful for her, climbing all those stairs. She couldn't walk without a stick and I think she was afraid of me. I must have been really terrifying. I had persecution mania and I thought everybody was a Gestapo agent except the people I had known before and once I did think of murdering her. We used to have rather terrifying conversations and we agreed to meet at the Brandenburger Tor ten years after the war had finished; we didn't. She left before the end and I don't know where she went.

We just existed. There was no heating; fortunately it wasn't a very cold winter. Curiously enough I don't remember being cold, although we did have ten or twelve degrees of frost and the temperature was rarely above freezing. Once, when we were taking Willi's clothes down to the N.S.V. for the refugees, walking back with Gerda, the stars seemed exceedingly beautiful. It was a clear frosty, moonless night and of course there was a complete black out so one could really see the sky. I can see why people used to think the dead go to heaven; they seem to have an affinity with the stars.

We had another very bad raid one night and a dud bomb fell in the garden right against the wall of our cellar. We all had to evacuate the building and went to the Hitler Youth Home which had a very good cellar. We were given coffee and very good sandwiches. We didn't forget them; Gerda went on talking about the N.S.V. sandwiches for a long time. In the morning I went back to the flat, although we weren't supposed to, and got some blankets and cooking pots. I took Gerda with me because I thought if I went up in smoke she'd better go too. In the afternoon the bomb was defused. It was done by prisoners, not political ones, just ordinary criminals; they got remission from their sentences for it. We were able to go home again. At least we still had our beds to sleep on. We had sat all day in the sun outside the Hitler Youth Home; it was early spring February, perhaps March. You sometimes get a warm spell like that in the spring.

Chapter 5 Berlin 1945

We could hear the Russian gunfire in the distance. One of the neighbours said you could hear it much louder in the suburbs to the east where she had been staying with friends. So one Sunday, nearly towards the end, Gerda and I went out on the Ringbahn, which still worked, and walked about in the forest. It was a lovely spring day, the trees were still bare, but the forest was warm. Gerda enjoyed that day in the forest. I thought we might get to the Russians; then I would be safe. I was quite convinced that the Gestapo was going to get me somehow. On the way home we went into a café and had something to eat. There were vegetable soups you could get off the ration. The food made me sick and I thought the Gestapo was poisoning me.

Then came the last raid. It was a daylight one and some of the time we stood out in the street and watched looking up at the blue sky. That was the end of that. Then the Russian barrage started. They were firing over our heads into the centre of town. It was a sickening noise that went on all the time and got on your nerves like tooth ache.

We took our beds down into the cellar with all the bits of candle we still had. The electricity wasn't working, so it was dark. We stayed in the cellar all day, only lighting a candle when someone wanted to find something. I went up and cooked potatoes on the balcony in a broken pail with wood we had collected from the bombed buildings and brought them down to the cellar to eat. Everybody else did the same, rigged themselves a cooking stove on their balconies. We were issued with special rations of coffee (two ounces, real coffee), rice and oatmeal, and were permitted to get the rations of sugar and fat for the whole four week period, if we could get it. We had to queue for it under fire and one or two people were killed queuing.

Water was still running in the cellar, but not upstairs. We settled down, if you can call it that, for the night and the lights went on which was much better. We could hear the Stalin Orgel.[1] I thought the S.S. would come round and finish off such as myself and was in such a state of nerves that I ate my precious coffee beans while I sat there waiting.

1 a Russian gun which shot off a lot of shells very quickly one after another

The children slept a bit. Then we heard the soldiers running in the street. We heard the Germans calling to each other, and then someone rattled at the cellar door and it opened. We all sat as if we had been turned to stone. A small Russian soldier came in and sat down in the midst of us. He took out his first-aid kit and started to bandage his finger. I went over and did it for him. We had a conversation, rather limited, as I can't speak Russian and he couldn't speak German. He gave Gerda a sweet, and he wrote something on a piece of paper and went away. It was a postcard I had been using to keep Gerda amused by letting her draw on it. It had a Hitler stamp on it and a few squiggles by Gerda. The Russian soldier had written: 'Now you are all safe and you will have democracy and the little girl will learn Russian'. I had it translated later. I still have it.

The Germans sat without moving. The saying 'scared stiff' is true. When he went out they came to life again. They had thought they would all be murdered. After that three more Russians came in. They were larger and they made the men give them their watches and they took the leather coat from our Nazi warden, he was the only one to have one. But the panic had gone out of us. Then seven or eight came in and took our blankets, lay down and went to sleep for an hour or two. They gave us back the blankets and went away. About ten o'clock the next morning some more came in and sat down and started to eat. They had bread and tinned pork. They gave the children slices of bread with the tinned pork on them. We hadn't seen such fare for many a long day. They put the N.S.V. sandwiches in the shade. Soon the grownups started to beg for some too and we were all given some; then these Russians went away too.

I thought they were going out of our street and I was afraid that the Germans would come back. So I took Gerda by the hand and with a blanket under my arm went towards Weissensee to find the Russians. I found some sitting in a cellar. I went to them and explained by signs that my husband was a communist and had been executed by the Nazis. They gave me a huge sausage, bread and some sweets and sent me with a soldier to the security officer. This was in a house in Weissensee. I sat in the living room of the house. There were some Russian soldiers waiting too and I got talking to them. One of them could speak a few words of German. He said he was from the Caucasus. He asked me if this was Berlin. I said, 'Yes'. He said, 'The Russians, the British and the

Americans would all come to Berlin, shake hands and go home'. He hadn't seen his wife for a long time and he wanted to get back to his farm. I saw the security man who spoke German. He told me I should be alright and to go home, but I could not believe him and waited to see him again. Some Germans were brought in and I started talking to them. I was curious to know what they thought about it. This made the Russian guard suspicious of me and, when at eight in the evening they were marched away, he sent me with them. I explained to the guard it wasn't right. He told me to go home and sort of shooed me away and at last I went home. I didn't tell the Germans in our flat where I had been. I expect they thought I had denounced them in the German manner which didn't improve our relations.

After that we were in no mans land for a week. The baker on the Prenzlauer Allee organised his own rationing system. We had to go in the morning to the back of the bakery and get a number, then in the afternoon we went for the bread. Each time we had to cross the Prenzlauer Allee. The Germans were still on the bridge and the Russians were down at the Weissensee end. They were shooting at each other from time to time. All the week a dead Russian soldier lay in the middle of the road on the tram lines. The electricity had given out again and so had the water in the cellar. We collected it from a tank built for the raids in the Grellstrasse. We boiled it on our rigged up stoves on the balconies. Once when I was fetching the water, I saw people looting the wine shop on the Prenzlauer Allee. The German soldiers had dragged the tin barrels containing spirits out onto the street and were shooting into them, I suppose to get rid of the stuff so that the Russians wouldn't get it and get drunk. But the people were swarming round with old medicine bottles and cups trying to get some of it as it ran out on to the street. Anybody would loot anything. When I was sitting waiting for the Russian Security Officer there was a cupboard in the room with linen in it. I took two towels. I made one or two expeditions to Weissensee, where the Russians were firmly established, to get some sort of help. The weather was fine and warm. I came onto a party of Russians cooking their dinner; they were burning a whole tree trunk. They had their horses tied up there. It looked absolutely incongruous in the Berlin suburb. They were quite friendly and gave us some food. I always had Gerda with me. On the way back we came onto a small hospital in the fields which was deserted. We walked through all the rooms to see if we could find anything. I found some spoons and surgical scissors and took them.

All this time the noise of the bombardment had gone on, a whistle and then a sort of sickening thud, and one felt one would give anything to stop it. It came shattering in all the time and brought on a feeling of nervous exhaustion like a toothache.

We went looting. The whole street went together. The first time it was a factory in Weissensee which had supplies of rye meal, sugar and bacon. I collected a pail of rye meal. Then we went to a factory on the Prenzlauer Allee. It had vegetables preserved in big tins but when we got home we found they had gone sour and they were no good. Then the word went round there was a train standing in the Weissensee goods yard and the Russians were letting people get on it. I rushed down with my pail and filled it with sugar. I ran back, found Fraulein Schneider and one of the neighbours. We took a pram and went off together. By this time there was a fighting mob round the train. Fraulein Schneider stayed with the pram to guard it and I struggled onto the train. I got about ten pounds of potatoes and then she went and got some sugar but by this time the Russians were turning people off the train. They fired a few shots in the air and we retreated.

The barrage had stopped and peace had come. We didn't really know what had happened. There were no newspapers and I didn't have a wireless. The electricity wasn't working so a wireless wasn't much use anyway. We just knew the barrage had stopped and the Russians were obviously in control. People said that the armistice had been signed and Hitler was dead.

I was still terribly worried about having a venereal disease. I had come to the conclusion that I couldn't be pregnant, although I had stopped menstruating. I suppose my middle class sex education had left me with appalling guilt feelings about sex. These I focused on the idea that I and the children had gonorrhoea. The children did have a certain amount of discharge. Whether this was caused by worms, which everybody had, the bad food or lack of soap, or whether they had picked up an infection from the Zuhlke children, who also had it, I don't know. Why I thought I had it was completely irrational. I didn't have any discharge and the old clap I had caught from Axel was cured by my abortions. Willi never caught it. The Russians had taken over a hospital in Weissensee and so I went there. Of course I took Gerda with me. They examined me, putting Gerda behind a screen during the process, and gave me some of those red crystals which seemed to be the universal cure on the continent for this type of illness. I was amused, while waiting, to observe a young and jolly Russian nurse cleaning the waiting room in the traditional East European manner. She took a mouthful of water and using her mouth as a spray damped the floor before sweeping. The shades of German hospital matrons must have got giddy in their graves. I also went to one of the emergency hospitals set up by the Germans in the air raid shelters. The doctor there realised what was the matter with me and gave me a sedative which I suspected was poison because it made me feel sick. While I was there two German women came in who said they had been raped by the Russians. I'm sure it was true. The doctor examined them, told them he thought they were alright, to wait for a week of two, and then come back for another examination. There was raping in Berlin, although afterwards it was enormously exaggerated. I once met a German later in London who, not knowing I'd been in Berlin at the time, told me that every woman in Berlin had been raped. It nearly happened to me twice. The first time was when the Russians came into the Gubitzstrasse. I was going up to cook my potatoes on the balcony when I found a Russian soldier on the stairs. He was going into the flats, presumably to loot. He tried to push me into one of the doors. At that time I was so pro-Russian and so taken up with my delusion of having gonorrhoea that I tried to explain this to him in sign language. I think he thought, quite correctly, that I was mad and desisted. The other time was in the Comandatura at Weissensee where I had to wait for a time. I found a Russian soldier beginning to loot our pram but I stopped him before he had time to take anything. There were a whole lot of soldiers sitting in the next room and they suggested I go in there, I think with this in mind. The sentry, who seemed a decent young fellow, told me not to go and shut the door on them firmly. I may be wrong about this and at the time it didn't occur to me. It was said that when the Russians first came into Berlin, they took the women out of the shelters and raped them. It took about three minutes; I think this was true. Nobody that I knew in our street was raped and, with the exception of the soldier I found on the stairs, none of the soldiers who came into our cellar tried to rape anybody. The Germans complained that they used the cellars as lavatories but then what does an occupying army do in a strange town? It's the open street or, if you prefer privacy, the nearest cellar. Vera told me later that it was much worse in the small towns and villages. It was also said that the Russians did have a lot of venereal diseases, particularly gonorrhoea.

There were notices posted up saying that foreigners could register at the Commandatura in Weissensee. So I went to find out about it. I always took Gerda and the pram with a few cooking pots. They sent me to a school in Weissensee which was full of Italians. The school had been used by the Germans for the army and there were cots in the classrooms. I found an empty one, a top one; they were in tiers one above the other with straw mattresses. The first night the Italians celebrated their freedom by having a concert party. They sang most beautifully until about two in the morning. The worst of it was that, if you wanted to go to the lavatory in the night, you had to climb down all the stairs in the dark and the lavatories were very dirty. I made several journeys home with the pram to get more blankets, cups and cutlery. It was a lovely walk along the lane at the back of the Weissensee cemetery, with the grass growing so freshly. I used to sit down on the grass in the warm sunlight and think. I always took Gerda and the pram with me. I was in a terrible state of mind. I didn't know if I was right to go away because Clara might come back to Berlin and find me gone. I thought I would be able to find out where the children were from the Americans once I got away from Berlin. I wanted to leave Berlin if I possibly could. We stayed three days in the school and were given three meals a day, mostly soup but with plenty of fat in it. On the morning of the fourth day, the Polish interpreter told us "Now you are all going home." So we packed our things and we started off. Everybody had a handcart of some sort or other; there was a huge, long stream of them. It was a lovely day in May. It was very strange to be on the march through the streets I knew so well. I was glad to go, taking nothing with me except what I could carry in the pram. Slowly the procession filed down the Berlinerstrasse to Weissensee station and under the railway, on down the Greifswalderstrasse to the Alexanderplatz. It was the first time I had been in the centre of town since the barrage. Mountains of brick, like knocked down ragged pyramids, pink in the sunlight, twisted tram lines, empty doors and windows of the façade of a house that still stood. One monumental stretch of ruins covered the whole centre of the town. Everything was still and at peace.

We marched on with the Italians singing and happy. Of the inhabitants, there were none to see. We came to a wine shop where there was wine in the cellars so everyone went in. I didn't as I wouldn't leave Gerda and the pram but the Italians gave me some to drink. It must have been about four o'clock in the afternoon when we came to a big square in the east of Berlin and halted. A red army officer, very tall, big and fair, addressed us in Russian, which was translated by another man. He said that any British or American D.P.s[1] were to step forward and they would be given special help. I moved forward with Gerda and the pram. I was the only one. The others filed on with their handcarts down the street. The commandant told me I could go into lodgings and wait to be sent back to England. As long as the mass of Italians moved along I was able to go with them but alone I had no strength. I asked him if I could go home and wait until I could be sent back to England. He said I could do that and keep in touch with the Commandatura. I cannot forget that scene. The wide German platz, not so badly bombed, and the afternoon sun slanting, the long file of Italians with their handcarts stretching out in a long line, and this Russian standing there addressing us. I turned my steps to the north-west. I knew vaguely where I was. I had a terrible feeling of helplessness and yet peace came into me as I pushed the pram through the ruined streets. I made for the outskirts of the city to go home by the circular road. There were grass allotments by the roadside. I came out at Weissensee and remembered that someone had told me that the vicarage had been turned into a home for American and British D.P.s. So I went along to see and, sure enough, there was a big placard with the words Amerikanske and Angelski. Before it stood a sentry with a long red beard. He looked as if he came straight out of Tolstoy. I showed him my passport and went in. Supper was being served and I sat down at the table. There was an Englishman who had been living in Germany and I didn't trust him. I thought he must have been a Mosleyite. His story was that he had been in Poland as a prisoner of war but he lived in Weissensee. We conversed, neither trusting the other. After supper the Russian commandant showed me a room where I could sleep but I had a feeling I must go home. I felt I couldn't leave my flat anymore so I told him I would come back in the morning and took the pram and wheeled it home. I had some rhubarb at home which had been bartered for some of my looted sugar. I felt I must go home and eat it. So I walked up from Weissensee to the Gubitzstrasse and put

1 displaced people

Gerda to bed thinking I should never have the strength to leave Berlin.

A few days later, as I was going out of the house to queue for bread, Clara walked in. She was quite alright and had brought some bread with her. She had been in Saxony. The children had been moved ever more to the west. When the end came and the American s arrived, they were somewhere in West Saxony. One day some Berliners arrived in the place, they were home guard men, and they had a lorry with a wood engine. They got friendly with the girls and suggested that they could come back to Berlin on their lorry, the idea being that they would get past the controls more easily with returning school children.

The schoolmaster was agreeable, so each took a rucksack, a blanket and a loaf of bread and started for home. The Americans let them through with no trouble and so did the Russians. They arrived at a suburb near Berlin, about twelve miles out. This was the home of the schoolmaster. He turned the children out of the lorry at four o'clock in the afternoon and told them to go home by themselves. They started off and luckily met some Germans who put them up for the night and sent them on their way the next day. They all walked together to Alexanderplatz, then they separated to go to their individual homes. Clara was ten at the time; some of the others were fourteen. I don't know what happened to the others.

Very soon after Clara came home things began to improve. We were issued new ration cards and the bread supply was sufficient to honour the ration so the terrible bread queues stopped. We also got real tea, and later, oil, meat and potatoes, but it was terribly little. In Weissensee there was a fruit and vegetable market and we used to go there to try and get some vegetables. The method there was that you waited on the market place until you saw a barrow coming in, then you ran to the barrow and fought your way as near as you could, and followed the barrow, fighting all the way to his stand. Then you had your place in that queue and you waited until he started to sell, sometimes an hour or two. You were lucky if you got something. It was no use joining a queue that was already there, as the stuff was always sold out by the time it was your turn.

The hydrants on the street started to work and it only took about twenty minutes to queue for water. The electricity came on, so we took to cooking on our electric heater turned on its side; there was no gas. All the people in our block of flats were mobilised to clear the streets and to dig a great pit in the communal garden for the garbage. This was done by each house having one person responsible to the block man, and he to the Commandatura.

The schools were started again. Our old headmaster called a meeting of all the parents. He told us that during the battle, when the Russians came in, Germans had looted the school of books and such like and he could not stop it. He stayed in the school and when the Red Army came he thought they would kill him. They asked him if it was a school and he said yes. They told him that within a week he must start the school again. They gave him two Red Army soldiers as guards and so the school was started again with our same teachers. They had very few books and practically no paper or pencils. Those who still had slates used them. The schoolmaster said that as a result of two years without school and the influence of the Hitler Youth, the children were undisciplined. He intended to discipline them again. He said that the Russians did no harm, and if any youngsters were caught making trouble, which would put the Red Army men against the Germans, they would be severely punished. He meant of course if the Hitler Youth started to be up to any tricks. The Germans had, before the end, propagated over the wireless the Werwolfe organisation. They were supposed to carry on partisan tactics, but there was no sign of this.

Many ex-Nazis managed to get positions on the Magistrat,[1] but I, a victim of fascism, failed to get any of the extra rations that I was entitled to. In fact many ex-Nazis managed to get extra rations. There was a Communist Party meeting. I went but it seemed lifeless. All the better comrades had been arrested, and the few, such as I, who were still there had suffered too much to be able to start to organise again. Now there were a lot of people who, in the past before Hitler came to power, had some faint connection with the left now became terrific communists. Of course all the time comrades kept on coming home from concentration camps but the long years of segregation and starvation had made them unfit to organise actively. They needed too much help themselves, many of them being terribly ill, to be of any use. I didn't attempt to take any part in the political life. I knew I was useless. I knew I had to get back to England and that this was my only chance of becoming normal again.

We had no wireless so we were dependent for news on the newspapers and rumours. All we had to cook was potatoes and we made pan-

1 Municipal Authorities)

cakes without fat out of the looted meal. We also made strawberry jam out of the strawberries in our garden without sugar; it was so inhuman always eating dry bread. I think the most horrible part of life was that we were so hungry we couldn't eat proper meals. We just ate the bread when we got it. I divided the loaf up into three parts and then we each had a slice from our thirds; sometimes I couldn't control myself and used to take a slice off the children's pieces. My ten year old Clara was wonderful. I suppose the children weren't quite as hungry as I was. Clara would bake little pancakes out of the rye meal and keep them for the next day. We had Russian time so it was light until eleven o'clock. Clara, with a band of little girls, used to go down to the Weissensee station where the Russians let them pick up the potatoes that had fallen on the ground when loading. They used to go at about eight in the evening and return at eleven with a little sackful. I used to wait near the station to help them carry them home. Sometimes the Russian soldiers gave them cheese. The children were out all day.

Then we read in the paper that the British and the Americans were coming to Berlin. I decided to wait till they came and then try to get back to England but I didn't believe they would come. I didn't believe I would ever get back to normal life. Then the Russian Commandatura told us we had to make eight flags: two Union Jacks, two Stars and Stripes, two Tricolour and two Soviet. These were to be hung, four at each side of the house. So the whole house got busy, using old sheets, old Nazi flags and any bits of stuff we had. The flags had to be big: about four feet by two feet. Of course we couldn't buy material and people were loth to give anything of any use but it shows the obedience of Germans that the flags got made, and when the order came, out of every house in Berlin, they hung. I went round on my bike to look.

Sometime in July the British and the Americans came into Berlin. I waited a week and then decided to go to the British for help. I started out in the morning on my bike with Gerda in a basket chair on the handle-bars. I cycled to Charlottenburg down the Ost-west Axe[1] and, when I came through the Tiergarten, I found some British soldiers doing something by the road. I asked them if they knew where I could apply to be sent to England. They said an officer was coming along and I'd better wait for him. He came along and was trying to explain something

1 a big road

to a German policeman so I translated for him. He said he thought I ought to go to the Deutsche Haus on the Adolf Hitler Platz. I asked him if he could send a letter to my father for me. He said he couldn't as it was against regulations, but if I could give him particulars he would write himself. I told him I was feeling desperate, that we hadn't enough to eat and that one of my children might be developing tuberculosis. He then asked me if I was hungry. I said I was. He had a jeep and he put me, Gerda and the bike on it, and took us to the regimental canteen. He gave me his address and told me to come to him if I was desperate. He seemed to me like an angel out of heaven. We went into the canteen and the soldiers gave us bully beef, tea, cigarettes and white bread with margarine, and some to take home. It was of course just like magic to talk English to English people once again. I went to the Deutsche Haus and spoke to a young soldier who told me to go to the American camp in Zehlendorf. I went home with the bread and bully beef and real margarine. When I got home I found Clara and we had a real feast. The bread looked like fairy bread and to have real margarine to spread on it seemed quite fantastic. The next day Clara took a piece of white bread to school to show her friends.

I decided to cycle to the American camp to find out if that was O.K. for all of us to go to the Zehlendorf Camp from where we could be sent to England. I had my persecution mania and I thought it was too good to be true. I left Gerda with a friend and went alone. It was a long way but I got there. I found an American officer and asked him if it would be alright. He said that as I was a German citizen it wouldn't be but, if the British had told me to go, perhaps it would be after all. I decided to go back to the Deutsche Haus and see somebody else. I was afraid we'd get into the camp and then be turned out, and not be able to get back into our flat as somebody else would have gone into it. So the next day I left both the children and told Clara to be ready in case we had to go. I went back to the Deutsche Haus which was a good hour cycle ride across Berlin. I chained the bicycle outside the Deutsche Haus and went in. I found the same soldier downstairs in the hall and asked if I could see somebody higher as I wasn't sure if it was O.K. He said all was fine but I could see somebody higher up if I liked. I went upstairs to the top floor and found a corporal. He was fair, with a thin nasty sort of a face. I asked him and explained everything and he said that it was not alright at all. I was lucky that my husband was dead but I would have to wait till a consul was set up in Berlin and then I could repatriate.

I went out of the room deciding that I couldn't wait for the consul and wandered about the building looking for somebody higher. I was standing outside a door and I could hear someone being interrogated in French. The voice of the interrogator sounded kind so I waited till the French woman came out and knocked. I was told to come in and found a man in a flying officer's uniform. He was dark with curly hair, rather fattish, with a nice face. So I told him the whole story. He was very kind indeed and said of course it was alright and could I get myself and family to Brandenburger Tor the next day at noon. He would get transport for me to the Zehlendorf Camp. I thanked him- another angel out of heaven- and went downstairs to bike home. When I got there I found that my bicycle had been stolen. I was terribly upset. I thought it was the Gestapo. I was standing there in despair as it was a good three hours walk home and I told the children I wouldn't be long. The same officer came downstairs and I told him what had happened. He said "Come along" and took me in his car. I got in and then he asked me if I had any information to give to security about the Gestapo. I said I had plenty. I thought I had but in reality I knew very little. We went first to the Tiergartenstrasse to security. Then he got another security man and another car and off we went. It was the first time a British car had been in the Russian zone, and he was very nervous but we went. I told him it would be alright. We drove up the Prenzlauer Allee, down the Grellstrasse to our street: two military cars, flying the British flag. They came upstairs with me. Clara was waiting with Gerda and had everything ready. She had put Gerda into a clean dress and herself into clean stockings with tidy hair. The two men took our stuff: a tent, two boxes and a pail, and we walked downstairs with them. The neighbours were looking out of their rooms, white to the lips, and when they saw us drive away they must have thought I'd been a British agent all the time. Of course they all had a hand in denouncing Willi so they were dead scared.

Chapter 6 Leaving Berlin

We drove back to security and I told the head man my story. Of course it wasn't much use really although it may have been good for them to experience the state of mind of somebody who had been against the Nazis in Germany all those years. They were very kind and gave us dinner and then the dark-looking officer drove us to Zehlendorf. He gave us chocolate, soap and cigarettes on the way to the camp. I stopped for us to call upon Vera Glass, who I knew had got back to Berlin. Lucy was there and was very pleased to see me. She was the first person who I felt really understood what I'd been through. The officer took us to the Zehlendorf Camp and left us there. I suppose it had been a slave labour camp. There were a lot of wooden huts, all full of French soldiers, but the huts were not too clean so we pitched our tent and decided to live in it.

It was lovely July weather and there was a swimming pool. The camp was full of French prisoners of war who were being repatriated. It was a wonderful feeling to be among the French prisoners; they were so happy. All the time a loudspeaker was calling out the names of those to be repatriated by air. The French did the cooking so of course it was good. There was a loaf of bread per person per day, soup twice a day and ersatz coffee. In the morning we went and fetched it in our cans and ate it in our tent.

The first thing was to delouse ourselves. We got D.D.T. powder from the French doctor. We washed our hair with the English officer's soap, put the powder on and then tied our heads with towels. With Gerda, whose hair was fair and very fine, one could see the lice running about her head. We were rid of them in a day. Vera and Lucy came to see us and promised that if we were, in the end, chucked out of the camp we could come to them.

The camp was in the forest. On the third day our names were called out. I didn't believe it but we were told to get into a great American lorry to go to Hanover. We climbed onto the lorry with a lot of French slave workers and drove off. It was about three o'clock in the afternoon. As we drove out of Berlin I thought that I had never believed we would leave that grim town. We drove on and on, down the Reichs autobahn, past Magdeburg. The American lorries were huge things and we could pull the apples from the trees as we passed. How beautiful the country looked. It was a showery, sunny day, and the dark shadows of the clouds and the sunlight raced over the landscape. It was about 1 a.m. and dark and raining when we reached Hanover. The camp was in a school with nothing but the floor to sleep on and that was dirty. We got permission to pitch our tent and slept there. The next morning we talked to a Pole. He said we had better go and report to the British officer in the camp and so we did. He took us to a house where the British were supposed to go which was just by the school. We were given breakfast there but it was so good, eggs and bacon, that Clara got diarrhoea. Then we were told we must report to the D.P.X. whatever that was. So they gave us a lorry and a soldier and we went to find the D.P.X. They were in the town hall but the man there said we must go to another D.P.X. somewhere else. We went there but it was Saturday and they were away. There was nothing to be done but to return to the camp which we did and came just in time for dinner. There were a lot of British there and they were very kind. They said we had better get onto a train going to Belgium. They took us in a lorry and put us onto the train. It was a cattle truck and there were Belgian and Polish slave workers on it. The Belgian Red Cross came round and gave us biscuits, milk and chocolate. The train rolled away and after a while it stopped in a field of corn; the corn had been harvested and was lying in sheaves. We climbed out of the train and collected sheaves to sleep on. The corn smelt so good that we ate the ripe ears and then we lay down to sleep.

I was still worried. I couldn't get rid of my fears. Why had the D.P.X. wanted to see us? I thought the Gestapo was still functioning and that they would still get us. All the same we had left Berlin, that was good, and we had food. We went on all night in the train and some time the next day we reached Bedburg on the Dutch frontier. Here we were all told to get out. We climbed out and carried our things into the camp which had been a huge lunatic asylum. It had been used in the war as a lazaret[1] by the Germans. It was a lot of separate houses in a wood. First we were put into a house with a Chinaman and an Australian and his wife who had been born in Germany. Then we were moved to the hospital which was run by nuns. It was one of the bigger buildings and was

1 centre for wounded and sick

still functioning as a hospital. It was full of Jewish girls from Belsen and Polish slave workers who were ill. We were given a room for the three of us and supper with milk. We stayed there about three weeks.

I will try to describe the people there as best I can. First there were the nuns, trying to do their best but, in a very difficult position as Germans trying to keep order with Polish and Jewish patients who wouldn't obey them. Then there were the Australians; they were a queer pair. Their story was that they had emigrated to Australia about 1913 or so, and had a farm there. In 1939 they were on a visit to Germany and had been caught by the war. It was probably true but I expect in the war in Germany they had told the Germans they were good Nazis. Can you blame them? They were afraid that the allied authorities would find out something they had done, perhaps in the war, perhaps they had worked for German security or such like. They were dead scared. But so were we all really. Then there was a Polish girl slave worker who was having an affair with a British tommy who had a wife in England. I think she hoped he would take her to England. Anyway he went on leave and I helped translate their letters. She wrote the letters in Polish, somebody else translated them into German and I translated them into English. We all did our best and the result was pretty good. Then his letters came back. I translated them into German and the other girl into Polish. I'm afraid she wasn't going to get to England but it kept her mind occupied. Then a Pole used to come and see them, a slave worker. The Nazis had brought him from Poland in a cattle truck and they had been packed so tight in the truck that by the time they got to Germany nearly all of them were dead. Then he had worked for a German farmer. (All the German women were crazy about the Poles, the good looking ones, and the Poles had to be very careful not to be found out, but equally careful not to offend their German mistresses who would otherwise have denounced them). Well, he had managed; he was a born adventurer, handsome and plausible. It was difficult not to like him. He was going to volunteer for some international police force or other.

The Australians tried to be friendly and we went to see them once or twice. I was very suspicious, distrusting everybody except the Polish slave worker, who obviously had nothing to gain or lose by us. The Australians gave me a pair of shoes and these I exchanged for a pair of boots for Clara at the local shoemakers.

Security came and we were all interviewed. I was again worried that we were not allowed to write to England and the security man seemed to be suspicious of us. I don't wonder; I was mad enough at the time to make anyone suspicious. I also had another worry. I was beginning to come out in huge spots that swelled up and were very painful. I thought again that the Gestapo was poisoning us and didn't tell the doctor. I had seen him once and told him that I thought we all had venereal diseases which the Gestapo had injected into us (mad enough). He said we hadn't, but I thought that is what the spots really were. Of course they were due to our bodies reacting to better food with fats after a long period of starvation and a lack of fats.

At last we heard we were moving. We were all loaded onto British jeeps, small and uncomfortable, and taken to a camp outside Essen. We went through Essen and it didn't seem to be so destroyed as Berlin. We arrived at the camp which was a lot of huts surrounded by barbed wire. We were issued with straw sacks. The Australians shared the same room with us. The huts had been slave workers' camps and they had not been deloused. In the morning we found we had all been bitten to pieces. We caught specimens and took them to the camp commander. They were bed bugs. Soldiers came round with D.D.T. and we were moved to another hut, away from the Australians, thank goodness. We seemed to be rid of the bugs too. We were only in that camp for three days but we made friends with a peasant family from the Baltic. When the Germans had retreated they had been more or less forced to go back with them. They didn't know whether to go back home or emigrate to South America. There were rumours that the D.P.s[1] were going to be settled in South America. They were not afraid of the Russians but they thought it might be better in South America, land of golden dreams. On the third day we climbed into British lorries and went to Munchen Gladbach, crossing the Rhine on an army pontoon bridge. The real bridge lay in ruins by the side of it.

Another thing happened in that last camp. In the middle of the night Clara had a bad dream and fell out of her bed. She was on the top bed and cut her face on the iron bar of the lower bed. We called the sentry and the doctor came and patched her up. In the same night all sorts of other people had bad dreams. Another boy dreamt he was at sea and must dive. He dived out of the top bed, his mother managed to break

1 displaced persons

his fall, but he was quite badly hurt.

On the third day the lorries came again and we were loaded into them with the Australians, Franco-Spaniards and other D.Ps claiming British or American citizenship. The Franco-Spaniards were Spaniards who had been working in Germany. There were also Republican Spaniards, who had been in concentration camps. We arrived at the Munchen Gladbach camp at about four o'clock. It was a housing estate just outside the town: two streets, about a quarter of a mile long, with new semi-detached houses. There were two flats in each house. We were to share the upstairs flat with another woman with two children. The Australians had the downstairs one. The other woman and I drew lots for which room we should have as there were two and we shared the kitchen. We were to be given rations and cook for ourselves.

This was the other woman's story. Her father had been a Hungarian waiter and had been working in England at the time she was born. Soon after, he had gone to Australia leaving his wife, who was German, to follow on with the baby. She didn't hear from him for some time, and giving up hope of being able to follow him out, went back to Germany. She never heard from her husband again. The child was brought up in Germany and when she was grown up she came to work in Berlin. She became friendly with a German who was the son of a furniture storekeeper. These two wanted to marry but the young man's father was against the marriage as she was only an ordinary working girl. She couldn't find out where her father had been born, and therefore couldn't get the necessary papers to prove she was not Jewish. Her mother did not know where her father was or where he had been born in Hungary. All this meant that she couldn't marry. They had three children: a pair of twins and a little boy. The father was called up in the war and she received family allowance from the Wehrmacht. Technically she was a British citizen. At the end of the war she had no more news from her husband. She lived near the Alexander Platz and in the bombardment of the city lost her home. She stayed for several nights and days wandering from one shelter to another. Then the neighbours advised her to apply for repatriation to England. She had her birth certificate, and went to the British authorities who put her, like us, in the D.P. camp.

She couldn't speak a word of English and she was in great fear that the British authorities would discover that, a month or two before the end of the war, she had taken out German citizenship in the hope of being able to marry properly. She asked me if I thought they could find out. I said I didn't think so as the whole place was destroyed and probably the records with it. Even if they had, they could hardly have turned her out of the D.P. camp. She was ill, having had a bad miscarriage just before the Russians came in. Like her, I believed that they would turn her out if they found out. I don't know what the end was. She had to go to the hospital and I refused to take her children on. Firstly because they had krätze, which I think is scabies, and because I realised that I was hardly capable of running my own children, let alone anybody else's. The camp commander arranged for a German girl to look after the children.

I got jaundice and it helped me get over the first part of my nervous breakdown. I had to chop firewood for our stove and this, with the jaundice, gave me such a high fever that it seemed to break a train of thought that had been running round my head all the time. I at last accepted the fact that I was forty. I'd lived quite a long time and that it didn't matter what happened to me personally. The children would probably be alright if I did conk out so I had nothing to worry about. Up to then, and all through the last year of the war, the feeling of having to go on as otherwise the children would just have died of want, had been weighing so heavily on me. Add to this the fear of being arrested any day, and the raids. Even after we got into the D.P. camps it was impossible for me to have any sense of security. Even though I was better, I still had a strong persecution mania. I always slept with an axe ready to hand in case anybody should come to get me.

We stayed in this camp for about five weeks and had many quarrels with the Australians. By this time I had made up my mind that they were in league with the Gestapo. Poor things, they were in much the same plight as I was. Each of us was equally suspicious of the other, and ready, if we only dared, to denounce each other of almost any crime. Once, when we were hauling up our wood with a string on a bucket, the Australian seized the string and broke it from the lower window. Gerda was pulling it up and her hand was cut. I ran downstairs and swore at them with every epithet I could think of and rushed off to complain to the camp commander, showing Gerda's hand which was bleeding. I give this episode to show the sort of things that happened.

We did make friends with a Dutch family. At that time I could bake with yeast very well. I baked her a birthday cake and we made friends.

She was a Dutch teacher. Her husband was German-American who had worked in Poland in German industry during the war. She taught German children there. She had become too humane to the Poles and was arrested and spent about six months in a concentration camp. They had three children. A school was organised by a Czech-American teacher. She was very nice and Gerda started to go to school to learn to read and write. Also we obtained a kitten. We had bartered it for some camp sausages with some Germans

At the camp the Franco-Spaniards arranged a wedding between two of their young people. There was much singing and goings on. Then security arrived to interview us. This was nerve wracking. We all made ourselves as respectable as we could and went up in turn. The Australians went in before us. I went in and stated my case. I was told that I could not be repatriated to England because I had worked for three weeks in a German factory. I said I didn't see this as fair. I had my people in England and could live there. My husband had given his life fighting fascism and I had more or less lost my reasoning. The security man told me it had been up to the highest authority so I said it had better go higher. However, I did get him to take the address of my father and, as he was going on leave, he promised to get in touch with him. This didn't worry me nearly as much as it would have done before my jaundice. When he came back from leave, all was well. He had met a friend of mine, who he also knew in England. It changed his whole attitude. I expect he didn't believe my story before. He was very understanding, realised my fears, and showed me all the papers to give me confidence. The whole thing was O.K. and we were sent off to Brussels the next day and then home.

I did believe the security man and we packed our things: the tent, two boxes, cooking utensils, tin cups and plates in a pail. While we were finishing up the Dutch children came. We gave them everything we had managed to collect out of the cellars of the empty houses: the axe, the saw and, some rations we hadn't used. We didn't want these things to fall into the hands of the Australians. We wanted the Dutch to have them. We gave our address to the Dutch and the Czech teacher but we never heard from them. We climbed onto the lorry with the Franco-Spaniards. There was a Spanish writer with his wife and child in the lorry and some workers. I sat in the lorry and looked at the faces of the Spanish workers, faces that came straight out of Goya and Velasquez, with a haunted sad expression in them. It made me feel how crazy the whole thing was. The Spanish writer gave us some cake left over from the wedding and I gave them grapes which I had bartered for some camp sausage. We came to the Belgian border and stopped there for a while. It was a sunny October morning, very fresh and crisp. The little town didn't seem to have suffered much from the war. The Belgian people were much better dressed than the Germans and already looked better fed. They looked very smart to us, but it was Sunday, so maybe they were all turned out in their best. I especially noticed the children who all seemed to have very smart shoes and stockings

We reached Brussels at about four o'clock. A Scottish tommy told us to get out. The Spaniards went on as they were going to another camp. The tommy helped us take our bags to a street corner and then we had to wait. Another lorry took us to a building in the centre of Brussels. We went up to the top floor and were interviewed by a British lady officer. She didn't seem to be very friendly but we filled in the forms and waited. While we waited a Soviet liaison officer came in. He complained that he could find nowhere to live. All the hotels were full of allied personnel and no arrangements had been made for the Russians. She was rather rude to him but I think she did something about it. I must say that she struck me as a rather snobby, disagreeable person, which I think she was.

However, as it was late, about seven o'clock, and we had had no hot meal all day. She did produce cups of tea but actually it was the orderly, working in the office, very kind and friendly, who looked after us. We were taken out by taxi to the camp. The taxi driver was Belgian. I had a long talk with him because we had to wait some time for our papers. He told me he had driven for the German High Command and had done a lot of private work driving loot for the German officers into Germany. He made no bones about it.

As we drove out to the camp, the streets were full of British and American army lorries and officers' cars. The camp was in a Belgian chateau. We were taken up to see the camp commander. He had a little room upstairs. He was a colonel, a Yorkshire man without a B.B.C. accent. We had a talk about D.P. camps in general and he was interested in my description of the camps we had stayed in. Then we went down and collected mattresses, knives, forks and plates. A German-American, a very tall lanky fellow issued them; he was friendly enough. We were given a room in a hut in the grounds of the chateau.

The next day there was a party. It was in honour of the golden wedding of the parents of the lanky American. It must have been organised by the Yorkshire colonel who had talked to me of the importance of organising the social life of the camp. Anyway, I went and made friends with a woman who was half-Indian. She was dressed in the most beautiful pale pink, muslin sari, trimmed with silver; it looked wonderful. She had been married to a German engineer in India but he had left her. Then I think she lived with another German and went to Germany. I don't know what she did in Germany. I had the feeling that many people had connections with security, had probably worked for both sides, but now were trying to persuade the authorities that they had only worked for the Allies. I still had my persecution mania. Probably they were just people who had been born in America or England, had been good Germans under the Nazis and now thought they had some claim to American or British citizenship. Very few of them seemed to have worked in the resistance movement or had been in concentration camps.

The American Red Cross gave us lots of things: jerseys and pyjamas and underclothes for the children, a dress for Gerda and a skirt for Clara. Clara was very pleased. The store was in the cellar and she tried on lots of things. The American woman who was doling out the stuff, and who I think was a Quaker, was very kind and seemed to understand the pleasure a child could take in looking at these things. She let her take her time. We went up to the doctor, who was Belgian. The children had impetigo. He put violet gentian on and asked me if I had had a nervous breakdown. I said I had but was better since having jaundice. I expect he noticed I was mad because I was very suspicious of him and thought he was a person not to be trusted.

At the end, when we were going away, I still had my pail. I could not part with it. It had done us such good service and I still did not know what was going to happen. Everything else we had collected, such as blankets and clothes, I gave to a German-American teacher who was going back to the Munchen Gladbach camp. We climbed into the lorry to take us to the airport. The doctor was there and he said crossly,

"What do you want to take this pail for? You are going on an aeroplane."

I said, "I have brought that pail all the way from East Prussia and I'm not going to leave it behind now."

I had very little idea of conditions in England. I didn't know if you could still buy a pail in England as you couldn't in Germany. I thought that England must have been hit far worse by the war than it was. It was hard to imagine that there were things to buy in shops. The camp commander came to say goodbye and shook us warmly by the hand. I had a good mark from him because I had voluntarily cleaned out the women's lavatories. Nobody else would do it because they were stinking and filthy. I only did it with water and wouldn't use a bit of blanket I had with me to dry the floors. I was afraid I might need it later.

Chapter 7 England

We arrived at the air traffic office in Brussels, unloaded and waited for the bus to take us to the airport. I was still afraid that at the last minute there would be a hitch. I saw a suspicious looking individual, who looked like a Gestapo spy, hanging around. He came and asked me a question but all went off alright, and we got onto the plane; it was a Dakota.

I'd never flown before; it is a wonderful feeling. The great machine goes down the runway and starts to lift. We landed in Croydon and were taken into the sheds. The immigration officer was very kind. There was nobody to meet us as they didn't know which day we were coming. My family had in fact been there the day before. The officer let me telephone but I couldn't remember the number and somehow could not remember how to spell the name or find it in the book. He arranged for an ambulance to meet us in Victoria. I had to give up my old British passport which I was sorry to do as it had served me well. A bus took us to Victoria. It was, as it often is in London, a slightly foggy evening but it didn't seem familiar to me. We got to Victoria and there was the ambulance. It took us to my mother and father's house. It was wonderful to see my relations again and to be at the end of my journey. However, I had a feeling that the Gestapo was still functioning and that there was something wrong.

The next day we went for a walk in Kensington High Street. The shops were full of the most beautiful materials; they looked like palaces. We went into Woolworths and the children bought themselves enormous bows to put in their hair. Also we bought some sweets. I stayed at my mother's for a week or two and then we thought it better to go and stay at my sister's in Hampstead. It was then that I really think I started to go mad. Up until then I had persecution mania which made me intensely suspicious of everybody. I started to have hallucinations. I felt all the time that the Gestapo were working and that they were still there. I was suspicious of everybody I met. I trusted to my instinct to decide whether they were good or bad.

Of course we had to do this under fascism in Germany all the time. Normally one waits to see what a person does or says before making a judgment about their character. I tried to sense it by watching people, studying their faces, seeing how they reacted in the slightest way to what one said. At any rate, one evening in November, we went to stay with my sister-in-law in Kent, and I think it was there that I first began to notice strange happenings. On the road there were notices saying 'All clear'. I thought they had been put there for me. Of course, in reality, it was where they had cleared some ammunition dumps. When we arrived there the house seemed so odd. On the landing was a chest-of-drawers and on it photographs of myself and my two sisters. I couldn't understand why it was on the landing. There was a green belt hanging on the bathroom door. Now in Berlin there was also a green belt hanging on the bathroom door. Of course it was just a coincidence. My belt was made of material and this belt was leather. All the same, I felt that someone was purposely trying to reconstruct my life for me. The photographs, the green belt, and the chest-of-drawers on the landing, somebody who I didn't know was staying in the same house. Also, I went for a walk and when I came home I saw two houses that I had never noticed before. I thought they must have been put up overnight. I must be a very important person and they were trying to show me how quickly they could build houses if they wanted to. I looked at the gardens, yes; the flowers were drooping, as if someone had just planted them.

Then I remembered how the security man had said, "It's been to the highest authority." Well, who was the highest authority? Why should my case have to go to him? I wasn't such a very important communist at all and never had been. Why should they bother about me? There must be one very high security authority who was against me and one who was for me, otherwise the one against me would have got rid of me ages ago. Who could the highest authority be?

I went back to my sister in Hampstead. One evening I was coming home along Well Walk and I passed a man. It was evening and dusk. I knew the man and he frightened me very much. He was the same man and had the same face as the German lunatic that Willi's brother Fritz had as a farm worker. I knew that he was not quite harmless. He had attacked Fritz once or twice. He had a terrible face, with a thin mouth and a mute but horrifying expression. The man passed me and gave me a look. I think about the next day we went down to Camden Town to buy some jerseys for the children but we couldn't find the shop and came home. We took the tube and as we came onto the platform the train went out and we were alone on the platform. Right away another train came in. It was completely empty but lit. We got in and, as we did so, three other men stepped in. I could see that they were all criminal lunatics. I sat quite still. At the next station other people got in and I could see that the danger had passed but I was terribly shaken. If the Gestapo were so strong that they could alter the trains on the tube, how could I alone manage against it? And I couldn't tell anyone as no one would believe me.

When we came home my sister wasn't in but I was quite sure there was somebody in the house. I was afraid they would show the children something that would frighten them. I mustn't let Gerda go upstairs alone. We all three sat in the kitchen and Clara started do her French homework. I managed to keep my mind occupied.

That night I didn't go to sleep. I was very sleepy but I wouldn't let myself sleep. I was afraid that whoever was in the house would do something terrible. A day or two before the lights had failed and an electrician had come to fix them. I was there alone when he came. When he had finished I paid him. He looked at my face and he turned white with fear. Why had he been so frightened? He must have done something wicked. When he mended the lights he must have fixed them so they would go on in the night and show terrible pictures. The following night I begged my sister to sleep upstairs in the next room to us. She did but in the night I heard her coughing and going into another room. I went into her room and asked her what she was doing. She said she had been asleep. Shortly after this, the children went to stay with my sister-in-law in Kent again and I went for a week to my other sister. Here I felt better. One day I went up to Swiss Cottage to see a German refugee who was returning to Germany. I had to wait about half-an-hour at the station. As I waited there I saw practically all the people I had known in my life. They came past me. How could the Gestapo have got hold of all these people and brought them from foreign countries? And why? Was it to frighten me? Was it to make me think of all the bad things I had done in my life?

By this time I knew that my sister didn't want me in her house. I tried to do everything I could to please her. As yet I had no money; I was still a German citizen and couldn't get work.

One day I came home and found that all the pictures in the sitting room had been changed round. It must have been the Gestapo. I thought that my sister would think I had done it in a fit of madness and that the Gestapo had intended her to think that. I quickly changed them back again. When my sister came home she said she had changed them herself and that we couldn't live there anymore. My mother was going to Ireland and we could stay in her Kensington house while she was away. Clara was to stay in Hampstead so that she could go to school there.

I had to accept this arrangement although I was loth to do so. I felt it would be a repetition of Berlin when I had been left alone with Gerda all that terrible winter. Gerda and I went to live in my mother's house in Kensington. It was an old house. We had the kitchen and sitting room in the basement and slept upstairs in my mother's room. I had to spend the evenings at home as I could not leave Gerda. One afternoon I went to the cinema. At the beginning of the film they showed a picture that was a still of the King and Queen. The King seemed to be smiling at me and he had a kind face. So it dawned on me that the highest authority is the King. The King must be helping me and preventing me from being murdered by the other security man. I thought I would go and have tea with the King and Queen. I took a bus to Hyde Park Corner and as I went along I saw the word 'Courage' written on the public houses. I thought that was written especially for me. When I arrived at Buckingham Palace I went up to a policeman and asked if I could go inside to look at the pictures. I told myself the King would know I was coming and arrange things. The policeman said that people weren't allowed inside except on special days so I went home again. I had taken Gerda with me. Another time I can remember standing in a crowded tube, near the door. Suddenly I felt that something very special was happening. I always felt that people were looking at me and they probably were. I must have looked odd. Anyway, a very intense feeling came over me, and I realised a man was standing next to me. I didn't dare look at his face. I could only see his hand which was very beautiful. As I stood there an electric current seemed to jump over from him to me. This thing was so intense that I moved away without looking at his face. When the next station came, everybody got out, including this man. Then I saw his face. He was very tall and he had a very white, very bad face with a drooping moustache. I could not believe it was the same man. I asked Gerda, who had been looking up at him, if he was fair or dark. She said he had a beautiful face and his eyes were blue.

After that the electric current seemed to keep on coming. I thought it must have been the King and that he loved me. I thought he must be a very good man and I must do everything I could to help him. A few nights after that I woke up in the night. I think the day was dawning and a most extraordinary feeling came over me. It was as though a shaft of light entered my body. It went through me and made me vibrate down to the very last nerve. I felt as though I was at complete peace with the universe. Afterwards I felt totally exhilarated. The next night I had a feeling that the King was in trouble and that I had to do something about it at once. It was about two o'clock in the morning and I telephoned the police. I couldn't tell them what I really thought because they would think I was mad, so I told them that someone was trying to get in the house. I waited for the police to come. The officer came in about five minutes and we searched the house. I told him what I really thought. I must say the police were extraordinarily nice about it. I suppose these things happen fairly often. They stayed with us, called my sister and waited until she came. They also got in touch with the mental hospital and an ambulance came about eight o'clock in the morning.

I understood what was happening. I had failed in what I wanted to do and I was going to be taken to a lunatic asylum. I suggested that everybody should have a cup of tea. I made the tea. There were two men with the ambulance and, after they had had tea, they said I was alright and went away.

In the meantime my sister had got hold of a friend of ours, who was a lady doctor, to come and talk to me. She persuaded me to go to a mental hospital to be examined. I agreed as I did think there was something wrong with me. At about eleven in the morning we went to Peckham House to have an interview with a doctor. I told him that I seemed in mental connection with somebody but I didn't know who it was and that it was upsetting my child. The doctor didn't explain anything to me. I had the impression that he wasn't a doctor at all but a mental patient and a wicked one at that. He was a very big man, rather fat, and he had very small, very wicked, pale blue eyes. Also I seemed to receive an electric current from him. It was very low and had a very short frequency, like a burring sound. My sister and the other doctor sat all the while, silent. They were as white as sheets. So I went into the hospital.

I had to have a bath but I didn't see why. And go to bed but I didn't see why either. I was perfectly alright physically. They brought us a beastly dinner with macaroni pudding made with milk. It was so nasty that I put it under the tray cloth; I was afraid not to eat it. I waited all the afternoon but I didn't see the doctor again. I thought I would be able to discuss all the phenomena which seemed to have been happening and perhaps find an explanation for them.

I didn't really believe in the King theory myself. It seemed too silly. I was an elderly, not very good looking woman. Why on earth should the King fall in love with me? But the doctor didn't come, and no explanation was given. I didn't like the hospital. Like all mental cases, I was very sensitive to atmosphere. I needed to be out in the air and getting impressions of nature all the time. Shut up in the ward, I was driven back on myself so I decided to make a dash for it. I thought, I'll try, I don't like this. I got out of bed and tried to get my clothes, but the nurse pushed me into a side room and locked the door. I was terribly upset. I tried to break the window to get out but they were made of unbreakable glass. After that they put me in a side room without windows. It seemed to me to be just like fascism again. Also they wouldn't give me anything to smoke and smoking was a sedative I desperately needed. However, I pulled myself together. After all this was in England; they couldn't starve you, and I was determined to fight my way out of the hospital some way or other. I decided to do physical exercises to try to keep healthy. Lying in bed and being inactive was a sure way of becoming ill. I also started to try and write poetry to keep my mind occupied. It was very hard to manage without smoking. I had cried all the first night and at last the doctor came and gave me an injection.

He was rather like the other doctor, only smaller, and with brown eyes. He didn't seem a wicked man to me. I thought and thought and tried to puzzle things out. I seemed to suddenly get ideas and one of them was that there are three sorts of impulses: the rational impulse, the unusual impulse and the irrational impulse. Generally one must follow the normal impulse but sometimes it is necessary to follow the unusual impulse. One must never follow the irrational impulse. As for the King, whether it was true or not, I couldn't be bothered with it. After a week in a mental hospital I had made up my mind that my freedom was more essential to me than a hundred kings. All the same I still had the feeling I was mentally in touch with someone and, when it left me, I was desperately unhappy. I felt that this person was not far off somehow.

My relations visited me. I said I couldn't stay in the hospital and, as I was a voluntary patient, I gave three days notice. I was determined that outside I wouldn't take any notice of my impulses or delusions, whatever they were. I needed to be free to walk about London and keep on seeing real things. London had seemed so divinely beautiful to me. I used to walk to Westminster Bridge and look at the panorama of buildings glittering in the sun. It seemed as if a veil had been withdrawn, and the whole marvellous unity of the scene was visible to me. I went to the theatre and to the picture galleries. It all seemed to be on an entirely different level and to have a hundred times more significance. But shut up in the hospital and locked in a room, I couldn't see things.

On the day I was to leave the hospital, my sisters came to fetch me. They told me I had to see another doctor down the road. We walked out of the hospital gates into the free air.

I said "Thank God, I'm out of that."

We took the tram to the other hospital to see the doctor. I told him that I had had delusions: I'd thought the King was in love with me and that I could make an atom bomb. I told him that if you were going to have delusions you better have really good ones but I would never have them again. We went out but my sister said we had to go back to get my things. When I got there I found that they had certified me.

I didn't fight physically. I knew it was no use. I said I'm going to fight this with everything I've got. I went back quietly into the hospital. It was pretty grim. I felt intensely bitter about my sisters and realised they would not help me. I had only myself to depend on. I asked to see a magistrate. I knew a certified lunatic could do this. The magistrate came and she seemed quite nice. She would keep asking me about the royal family. I told her, that to my knowledge, I had never had anything to do with them. But it did no good. I was locked into the side room. I wanted to go to the lavatory, but nobody came. So I thought I'll rouse them, and I beat an imitation of the Berlin barrage on the door. After that they took me to Ward No. 3. I had to get into a chair and be wheeled there even though I could walk perfectly well. Again I had to get into a bed. I was in a long dreary ward, rather dirty. In the beds lay women, some still, some screaming and shouting, some free of all their clothes and naked. There were two chair-type lavatories in the ward and they stank. I realised what I was in for and became hysterical. I said I'm only an old woman; I don't need this. I screamed for about six hours and asked for an injection. At last the doctor came and gave me one. I had a good sleep and the next day I started to try and study the patients. I got up and did physical exercises until the nurses let me dress. I also helped them clean the ward.

Opposite me lay a woman who was so thin that she looked like a skeleton. She always seemed to be taking off her clothes, perhaps for the purpose of washing or going to the lavatory. Her terribly emaciated body was a grim sight. She called every five minutes or so for her husband.

Then there was a dark handsome girl in what they call a siren suit. This is a sort of pyjamas made in one piece and fastened up at the back. It goes right over the feet and is striped, like pyjamas. It is for patients who continually tear off their clothes and rip them up. She was always going into extraordinary positions. One could talk with neither of these.

Then there was a girl who had been a medical student. You could talk to her. I soon realised that she would talk sensibly as long as she identified me with someone she had known in the past. As soon as the conversation or behaviour differed from that character, she went away. This gave me a clue to my own illness. I realised that when I had seen all the people I knew on the station at Swiss Cottage, my brain, suffering from shock, had identified types as individuals. People do run in types. My brain, through shock, didn't take in impressions properly and mixed things up. I thought that the person of more or less the same type was the actual person that I knew. Also it occurred to me that I hadn't seen all the people I knew. This would be explained by the fact that their type had not appeared on the station. I still couldn't explain the mental communication I had felt with certain people such as the King. I suppose it was a sort of schizophrenia, or split personality and that I was of course communing with myself.

Another patient was very tall and rather wonderful looking. She had continual inspirations and every few minutes would jot something down. She showed it to me; it was mostly disconnected words. I suppose that was schizophrenia too. I couldn't and still cannot explain the phenomenon of the electric current or the burning sensation.

I do not understand how we knew the doctor was coming down the ward long before there were any visible signs of him. I explained it to myself in this way: in some mental illnesses some of your subconscious mind sort of gets conscious, and that one has the same senses as animals. It is also true that wild animals are less afraid of lunatics than other people; at least it seemed to me to be so. The head doctor, who was a very kind man, did once have a sort of explanation. He said that your herd instinct is responsible for some of the things that happen.

The food in Ward 3 was very bad. The patients in bed were fed with tea in a plate, with bread soaked in it. Our food was better. I think they put something in the tea, like soda, to keep us fairly low. It may just have been that they didn't clean the teapots properly. It had a nasty taste and of course I imagined the other thing. I will stop trying to make observations and will continue to tell the facts as well as I can. However I will say one more thing. At no time, except once when he visited me much later at the other hospital, did the doctor offer to explain to me my illness. We were not allowed books on psychology, nor did they seem at all interested in trying to find out why we thought the things we did think. Altogether my impression was that although the treatment was not intentionally cruel or unkind, it was still based on the good old principle of punishment. If you became hysterical, you were punished for it.

It seemed to me that I was fighting the Gestapo in the hospital, and the misery that I encountered did two absolutely necessary things for me, without which I do not think I could have been cured. Firstly, it put a hill before my mountain, and so gave me a perspective on it. Secondly, I was able to re-enact in the hospital my struggle in Germany. I think that is what a mental patient suffering from shock has to do. I had come from long years of horror in Germany pretty suddenly to utterly different conditions in England. The best thing for me was to be put back into the nearest thing to fascism one could find and work slowly out of it by one's own effort.

There was another fairly intelligent patient on the ward, a youngish quite good looking woman. I think her story was something like this. She had been married to a man she didn't love and had fallen in love with a young soldier who had been killed at Dunkirk. The shock of it had driven her mad. She used to go about singing 'For there's something about a soldier'. She desperately needed sexual intercourse, as we all did, and had turned lesbian. She and I made friends, and she started to show me how to be a lesbian. I found that I could make it work but I didn't want to turn lesbian. So I told her we were both grown women and ought to be able to manage without that sort of thing, and I wouldn't do it again. But she kept trying.

Another patient was called Annie and she wore a siren suit. She had a certain natural gift for being funny and making rhymes although she couldn't talk sense. We used to sit there and make up rhymes together.

Afterwards she developed a dreadful abscess on her back. I suppose it was a result of the long years of bad vitamin-less food. It got as big as a pudding basin. The doctor came to lance it. He did it without an anaesthetic. I lay and watched her being cut. By this time I had been moved across to the bed where the thin woman had lain; she had been put in a side room. There seemed to be a curious tradition and ritual about which bed one was put in but on what it was based, I couldn't find out.

There was one thing which I must not leave out. One of the night nurses was an English woman, a real old Londoner. She had worked in the hospital all through the war. She had two cats which, when she came on duty, marched sedately after her into the ward. She had the kindest heart and the most wonderful human personality. When she walked into the ward all was peace. I always woke up at about four o'clock. She used to sit by the fire and my bed was next to it. We talked about all the old music hall stars and actors and actresses of my young days. She always gave me two cigarettes every morning, one at four and one at about six. It made all the difference. She must have paid for them with her own money. She seemed to me a human being in a world of madness and when she came into the ward I could feel I was in England.

The doctor told me I was to be sent to another hospital. This upset me very much. At least I knew what to expect at Peckham House. I had managed to organise a few privileges for myself and had got the hang of the nurses and could deal with the worst one fairly successfully. But a new place meant that everything had to be built up again. God alone knew what the nurses and doctors would be like. I begged and prayed them to let me stay at Peckham House. Also, at least I was in London and the feeling of it was homely. This one was in Northampton, a place I didn't know. But it was no use.

One fine day a car came to fetch me with two nurses. As we drove northwards I seemed to feel the atmosphere change. In London everybody was awake and conscious of things. I still thought that they knew me but, as we went north, it seemed as though people were less conscious. The nurses weren't too bad and they didn't seem to mind me smoking. We reached Northampton about four o'clock and drove into the hospital which was just outside the town. It was originally a gentleman's house but for the last hundred years had been an asylum. We drove through big, well kept grounds, past the main buildings. It looked grim enough, mad enough, with figures at the windows. But we passed it and went to an annexe called Wantage House. It looked modern and quite bright. I went inside to the waiting room and waited to see the doctor. After a while we came in. His name was Gibson. He was a ginger-haired man of middle height, rather thick set. I didn't much like the look of him and was feeling very tense as a result of trying to adapt myself to the atmosphere of the new hospital. So when he finally examined me I was very hysterical. He asked me what I could do and I said I could do almost anything. He did his tests. I asked how many cigarettes I was allowed a day and said I had ten in the last hospital. He said I could have twenty. I said that was fine and thought well, if I can smoke I'll be alright.

We went into the ward. It was a long room with a glass veranda down one side and the beds all in one row. It was certainly much cleaner than Peckham House. Nobody was naked or having an epileptic fit and there were no lavatories in the ward. I felt very strange. I had to get into bed as usual. Why they do that I don't know. To be put in bed when you are in an intense nervous state of excitement and, to somebody who hardly ever goes to bed, is one of the hardest things I know. They brought me my tea but no smokes. I was keyed up to bursting point and desperately needed it. I asked the nurse and told her the doctor had said I could have twenty-a-day. She said she didn't know anything about it. Some of the other women were smoking and since I couldn't, I started to sing. I always did this when I was nearly at breaking point. That did the trick. They lumped me off to what was called the silent room at the end of the ward. The silent room was divided into two sorts of cells. In one was a proper window and in the other only a high up one. There was a bed in each room but no other furniture. In the door there was a peep hole for the nurses to look in. The door was constructed with a bolt outside in the floor so that it could be left ajar. The person inside couldn't get at the bolt. It was clean and smelt all right. I thought, well it's better to be alone. Also one of the nurses was kind enough to give me a cigarette so I settled down as best I could.

They came and gave me some dope which I think it was paraldehyde. I took it to see what it was like. It sent me to sleep but, when I woke up in the morning, I didn't feel as if I had slept and my brain felt stupid. I decided not to have any more dope. I spent the day doing physical exercises and singing. I took off my pyjamas to do the exercises as I didn't want them to get all sweaty. I also tried to find out something about the woman next door. I couldn't get much sense out of her. I think she asked me if I was the original Joan of Arc. I said I was original alright.

Those three days were very trying. I began to half believe in the King theory and the Gestapo theory. I supposed that the King was a good man, had fallen in love with me and needed me. They wanted to do him down and had started to try and drive me mad in order to get rid of good elements that might support him.

Why shut up someone like this? I was obviously in a state of intense nervous excitement. Why put someone, who had such frightful memories they were trying to forget, into a room with nothing to do, nothing to take one's mind away from things? Solitary confinement seems hardly the best way of caring for someone on the verge of madness. It has often been known to drive people mad. But that seemed to be the method and it didn't make sense to me. However, I had one comfort. The window of the cell looked out onto a shrubbery and I watched the birds a lot of the time. They soon put a stop to that and came and put shutters on the window. I felt I must see something to take my mind off things so I climbed onto the bed and looked through the tiny gaps in the shutters. They took the bed away so all I could do was to sing and exercise. I also had a pen and paper. I wrote out a memorandum for the doctor on what I thought mental patients needed for their cure: a very regular life with some sort of social employment. All the rules must be very carefully explained so they shouldn't mix up some of the rather peculiar rules with their delusions, as I had done. I found out afterwards there is a hospital rule about going to bed for the first three days and not being allowed matches for fear of fire. Also that mental torture was quite unnecessary as a mental patient had plenty of that already. I handed this to the doctor when he came to see me. He obviously thought that it was just another bit of madness. Anyway they kept me in there three days and nights with the windows shuttered and I managed to keep from going quite mad by singing and doing physical exercises all the time. I had come to the conclusion that it was much better to do the things which made the doctor think I was mad if it helped me to work off my excitement.

After three days of this they let me out. When I got out I was allowed to go outside and sit in the sun. The trees looked all crooked, so I realised my vision had been affected. After about six hours this righted itself. The solitary confinement did me a lot of harm because after this

I began to have many more curious sensations.

I had, however, managed to get out of having the dope. I fought every time they gave it to me. There were six or seven of them and they tried to force it down me but I spat it out. If I did swallow any I did physical exercises to get it out of my blood stream. After three tries they gave it up. I was quite sure that if my mind was doped I wouldn't be able to think things out. If I couldn't do this I would not get well. After this I did at least get enough to smoke. I suppose it dawned on the doctor eventually that this was the form of dope I took without trouble. Another medicine I asked for was cod-liver-oil. The doctor thought I had a delusion about it. The only delusion I had was that I thought it would be good for me. In my bad nervous state I thought it was a good thing to build oneself up physically. The doctor didn't get this idea. It was not until about five months later, when an aunt of mine very kindly visited me and brought some, that they allowed me to have it. I couldn't help thinking that even if the doctor was right, and it was a delusion, it was rather a good one for a mental patient. It certainly couldn't do any harm. By this time I had come to the conclusion that the method was to give all the patients the wrong treatment and medicine. If anybody gets better, they must be very healthy.

Another example of the very curious attitude to mental patients was this. We had an occupational therapy class and I asked if I could have some wool to knit a jersey for my little girl. I had some clothing coupons and asked if the occupational therapist could get some for me. She said she couldn't but she gave me lots of little balls of wool. These were not nearly enough to knit a jersey so I devised a pattern in which I could change the colours all the time and make it look nice. It was very difficult but I did make a very attractive Fair Isle jersey. Of course they thought the jersey meant something special to me. It didn't; I was just trying to keep my feet on the ground by making something for my own child. If the occupational therapist had given me enough wool at first, I wouldn't have made such a complicated pattern.

Well, life went on, not so badly. I made friends with the other women in the ward. They were none of them very interesting cases and all too terrified to talk about their delusions. I, myself had very bad delusions. I seemed to be sensitive to all kinds of electric streams that went through me. I thought I must be linked with thunder, and that by clapping my hands I could make thunder happen somewhere. This seemed to get worse at different times of the day. If I touched certain metals and woods I could insulate myself. It helped if I ate a lot of stodgy food.

The food in Wantage House was good. The ward was scrupulously clean and most of the nurses, I think there were only two exceptions, very kind; especially one nurse whom I even trusted to try to begin to explain my delusions.

I was sent to the main building, Ward 3. The ward sister met me at the door. She was very dark and I just stopped myself saying, "Have you used Pears soap?" I went with her into the ward and there we received some wonderful nursing. Her name was Sister Maloney and she was a very good mental nurse. She never, if she could help it, refused us anything. She always had a cigarette for me if I asked. The result was that we were all of us devoted to her and would do anything she wanted us to do. Ward 3 was much more interesting. We had all the bad cases and there was a lot to observe. Sister Maloney noticed that I was quite a good mental nurse and she let me go into all the patients and try to find out what they were thinking. When I arrived in Ward 3 they did not put me to bed or lock me up for three days, also they allowed me to smoke. The result was that I did not get hysterical the first night.

Sister Maloney sent me in to see one of the patients. She was a tall blonde, very good looking, former A.T.S. girl. She was sitting on a chair and on a table by the window was an arrangement of flowers. Stuck onto the flowers were cuttings of newspapers with words on them like, 'Where are we going?' or something like that. I realised that with the bits of paper she was trying to establish an atmosphere of her own. She had cut bits out of the paper, sentences which seemed to be appropriate to her, and they were. Her name was Joan and we became good friends and kept each other company. She had been married to a man who had deserted from the Navy. When he had deserted she had gone down to Plymouth to try to see him and help him. She had waited for him all day but he would not see her. Finally she went home again. She was only a voluntary patient and was having insulin. The two of us used to organise our morning tea if the duty nurse was friendly and allowed us to do so. We went to bed at eight o'clock and it was a terribly long night. Early morning tea was a joy indeed.

We had our tea and smoke in the morning. A friend of mine, who had been in a mental hospital and knew something about it, sent me painting materials. I started painting. Sister Maloney encouraged this.

I cannot remember how the sensation of electricity currents died down. I only know that Sister Maloney's organisation of the ward made it possible for me to take a lot of interest in the other patients. By never locking me in and always allowing me to smoke when I wanted to, she stopped me from getting hysterical.

There was a girl there who was a W.R.E.N. At first I identified her with Himmler but I pulled myself out of this. I took her into my room, gave her cigarettes and let her listen to my wireless, which the doctor had allowed me. She used to sit there and say,

"It's not me; we're in Colombo."

Human companionship and comfort did her a lot of good. The result of this was that my mind was occupied and I had the feeling that I was doing a useful job in the hospital. I had taken a lot of trouble with both Joan and Nell (the W.R.E.N.) and they got better. This gave me an interest in life, and the sensations got less. The doctor kept on bothering me about the King, until I said,

"As far as I'm concerned, the whole Royal Family can go to hell and stay there."

I don't know if that convinced him.

There were good things about the hospital. We had weekly dances. At certain times we were allowed to walk alone in the gardens and we could make friends with the male patients who were allowed out. That helped a lot. At the dances the doctors used to turn up in full evening dress; it was compulsory. In the end I even made it up with Gibson, more or less. I think he was really trying but I think he got my case wrong.

I made friends with a patient in Ward 2, called Mrs. Suffolk. I think it had been an air raid that had done for her. She was rather like me in a way. I mean we both always worked hard in the hospital, washing up and cleaning the wards. We did it for two reasons: firstly to keep our minds off things and also to keep on good terms with the nurses. It saved them a lot of time. She also had a very peculiar hair style. I don't know whether she had a leucotomy or a bad head wound caused by an air raid. I now suspect that it was the latter. Anyway, she combed her hair from the back over to the front of her forehead and tied it round with a black velvet ribbon. We both of us had rooms on the top floor of ward 2. In the evenings we had to leave the ward and go up to our rooms. They were cold, but we were allowed to keep the doors open. We used to make cocoa out of tinned milk, which we bought with our own money, and cocoa powder mixed with hot water from the hot tap. She often came and sat in my room to listen to the wireless. She obviously had the same delusions as I had about electric currents going through her. Her explanation was that it was the B.B.C. doing a sort of special stunt of listening in to the hospital. I suggested to her that she should have insulin. I said it seemed very harmless and if the doctor could say he had done something for you, he'd be more likely to let you out. But she wouldn't trust it. She thought the hospital was fairly good and there were good influences working in it, one of these being Gibson. She didn't trust our doctor in the main building.

At any rate, I went into Mrs. Suffolk's room one morning; I think I wanted to give back a poem that she had written. She shouted at me. She said I was sneaking in because I wanted to see her head. I went very quickly.

Then there was another patient, a farmer's daughter from Leicestershire. I can't remember quite how I made friends with her but probably because she was from Leicestershire. Anyway, I'd managed to get the privilege of making myself a cup of early morning tea in the Ward 2 kitchen. She was mostly up early and she was allowed out of her room. One morning I took her up a cup of tea. She was looking very worried and suddenly she seized her hair, which was a wig, and showed me her naked scalp with one long strand of white hair trailing from it. I was staggered as I had no idea that she had a wig. The expression on her face, the desperation in her eyes, and the naked bald head on the top, stood me riveted to the ground. She put it on again. I said,

"Do you mind taking it off again for a minute, then I'll get used to the idea you wear a wig." She did so. After that I began to wonder if everybody in the hospital had wigs. I went round asking patients I knew well enough if they would mind if I pulled their hair to see whether it came off or not.

A very attractive looking Danish girl came into Ward 2. She had been engaged to an airman who had been killed and then, I think, to another airman who had also been killed. After that she tried to commit suicide. She was with me in Ward 2 for a while. Then she went to Ward 1, which was more comfortable, but she got worse and was sent to Ward 3. I asked sister Maloney if I could visit her, so I went along. She was lying in the ward, that awful ward, where the atmosphere seemed to hang over you like a dream, and she was in bed. I was terribly shocked to see her.

Her hands were crossed over her knees, and she was sitting up in bed. Her face was mottled and yellow and the bones all stuck out. She was terribly thin and the expression on her face was such that I could see in her mind that she was passing through the worst. I sat beside her for a while and gave her a cigarette and then came away. She didn't talk, but she got better.

There were two epileptic cases in Ward 3. One of them was a girl of only 14, the other was 18. That was a very terrible thing to see. At eighteen the girl had a life sentence. When she wasn't having fits she was quite sensible but she had to live in that atmosphere all the time. She was never to know any other life. It was also terrible for the fourteen year old. She only had very mild fits but, to be put in with all those women, to have no chance of learning anything, seemed to me to be terribly wrong. When she began to realise what it meant she became very hysterical which was bad for her. I believe her mother did take her away in the end.

I was let out in the early spring and my sister came for me. We went to the station. It was a dampish cold day with a little snow on the ground. But how friendly was that station and how human it seemed, then the train going through the country side, and then old London. I went on by myself to my sister-in-law and stayed there for a while.

Finally I started to pick up the threads of a life, broken by seventeen years in Nazi Germany and one year in a British Lunatic Asylum. I felt I had no friends but I was free.

Left: Photo of gravestone in a Bremen cemetery put up by Willi's parents. The carving and lettering was designed by the architect Hannes Meyer, Bauhaus Director and head of the Building Department 1928 -1930. Sadly the gravestone no longer exists. It was probably removed when his parents died.
Right: This is a brass plaque, about 4 inches square, embedded in the pavement outside the Gubitzstrasse apartment building. It is called a 'stolpersteine' and you can find them all over Berlin. They mark the living places of men and women who fought against the Nazis.

Endpiece

Biddy went on to lead a full and active life. She lived in Acton, a suburb in the West of London. Biddy changed her name from Jungmittag to Youngday as it made life easier not to have a German name after the war. In the 1950's the German Government gave her a lump sum and a pension for life as restitution money.

At first she remained a member of the Communist Party but after Hungary she joined the Labour Party. She was active in the C.N.D. movement, being one of the original members of the Committee of 100 along with Bertrand Russell. After a sit-in demonstration in Parliament Square she was imprisoned for a month in Holloway.

She was involved in the local community and one project involved constructing an adventure playground on the South Acton Estate in the 60's. She made a delightful film about it. Every week she taught Art at the Saturday Morning School for the West Indian Community.

She continued to paint throughout her life producing oil portraits, water colour landscapes and clay sculptures.

She died in 1987 at the age of 82 surrounded by friends.

Willi's wish for his children was fulfilled. Clara studied Medicine at the Middlesex Hospital and became a Professor of Endocrinology specialising in diabetes at St. Thomas' Hospital. Gerda read Agricultural Botany at Reading University and taught Science in Kenya, Tanzania and Jamaica as well as in England.

The resistance against the Nazis has not been forgotten. In 2009 an exhibition was held at the Humboldt University in Berlin about the Saefkow-Jacob-Bästlein Organisation. There are brass plaques (stolpersteine) in the sidewalks in Berlin commemorating the sacrifice made by men and women like Willi Jungmittag.

Willi's brass plaque is in the sidewalk outside 47A Gubitzstrasse.

HIER WOHNTE
DER
ANTIFASCHISTISCHE
WIDERSTANDSKÄMPFER
WILLY
JUNGMITTAG
GEB. AM 8.4.1908
ERMORDET
AM 20.11.1944
Tafelerneuerung 2010
WILLI JUNGMITTAG erlernte in Bremen den Beruf
des Schriftsetzers. Von 1928 bis 1930
studierte er Fotografie am Bauhaus in Dessau,
wurde Mitglied der Vereinigung der Arbeiterfotografen
Deutschlands und trat der KPD bei. Anschließend
reiste er als Fotoreporter durch Europa.
Nach der Machtübernahme durch die Nationalsozialisten
fand Willi Jungmittag in Berlin Arbeit
als technischer Zeichner. Er beteiligte sich am Widerstand
der Saefkow-Jacob-Bästlein-Gruppe.
Im Frühjahr 1944 versteckte er in seiner Wohnung
den flüchtigen Hamburger Kommunisten
Bernhard Bästlein. Nach seiner Verhaftung im Juni 1944
wurde Willi Jungmittag am 7. September
zum Tode verurteilt. Die Vollstreckung des Urteils
erfolgte im Zuchthaus Brandenburg.

Here lived the antifascist
resistance fighter
WILLI JUNGMITTAG
Born 8.4.1908
Murdered 20.11.1944

Willi Jungmittag trained as a typesetter in Bremen. From 1928–1930 he studied photography at the Bauhaus, Dessau, becoming a member of the German Photographers' Union and the German Communist Party. He subsequently worked as a photojournalist in Europe. After the takeover by the National Socialists, Willi found work as a technical draughtsman. He took part in the Saefkow-Jacob-Bästlein resistance group. In spring 1944 he hid Bernhard Bästlein, a communist from Hamburg and an escapee from prison, in his flat. After his arrest in June 1944, Willi was sentenced to death on September 7th. The sentence was carried out in Brandenburg prison.